Places in the Book of Acts

By Dr. Randall D. Smith

**To my many travel-study friends for the hours of joy
on the journeys through the Bible lands**

Table of Contents

Alphabetical Listing

This handy reference lists places alphabetically and are generally spelled as they appear in the text of the New Testament (King James Version). If the name appears unaccompanied, assume it is a city of the ancient period. The regional names and islands are specified after the name, but were the designation of a geographical area in the Book of Acts. In some cases modern names follow the Biblical name to help students.

Achaia (Region)

The region of today's southern Greece, Achaia was a name used in a variety of ways in antiquity. Homeric epics used the term Achaeans in the way we would likely use the term "Greeks". In Hellenistic times, the Achaean league or confederacy desired each republic to remain free and equal, but the confederacy succumbed to Roman ambition in 146 BCE.

The Romans refined the term by using it for the senatorial allotment of the southern portion of the Greek Peninsula (hence a proconsul represented the seat of Rome, cp. Acts 18). Though some government functions were maintained during Roman times in Argos, as a leftover of the older confederacy, the more important functions were placed at Corinth. Churches of Corinth and nearby Cenchrea are certainly of Achaia, and these groups are inferred in references of the New Testament (2 Cor. 1:1; 9:2; 11:10). Because the "household of Stephanus" was considered by Paul as the "first fruits of Achaia" (1 Cor. 16:15) we see that he uses the term as centered at Corinth. Generally, he probably viewed Greece as two provinces, Achaia in the south and Macedonia in the north. It is generally agreed that the use of "Greece" in Acts 20:2 is actually a reference to Achaia. Best manuscripts of Romans 16:15 indicate the term "Asia" is probably the proper transmission, and not "Achaia" as other texts indicate.

Today the term refers to the area south of Thessaly (central Greece) including the Pelopponese, the Cycladic islands (over

220) and the area surrounding Athens, south of the Euobean Island. The mission work of Paul in the area is reflected in Acts 18 and 19; with specific mention from Rom. 15:25ff; 1 Cor. 1:16, 16:15-17; 2 Cor. 1:1, 9:1-2.

Amphipolis

Acts 17:1

Paul passed by the supply-city of Amphipolis on his Second Missionary journey on his way to Thessalonica from Philippi. Some scholars pose the possibility that Paul lodged overnight there, as part of a three-stage journey from Philippi to Thessalonica, but the text is not specific on this point. There is no record of his preaching there, and there was little tradition of a community of believers from the apostolic ministry. It is likely the city was not evangelized until a generation after Paul, but nevertheless became an important Byzantine Christian site.

Amphipolis was already one of the most important cities in ancient Macedonia. One ancient historian reported it was founded by the Athenian General Hagnon (son of Nicias) in about 436 BCE near a village called Ennea Hodoi. Thucydides also (History, 4:102) claims that Hagnon gave the city its name because "It was surrounded by the river Strymon which nearly encircled it." Amphipolis may be translated *a city pressed on all sides*. It grew as an important trading center with Thrace and the village of Ennea probably became its port – though renamed Eion.

In the following century the city became independent but was soon taken up by Philip of Macedon as he expanded his power grip on Macedonia before moving south to control all of Greece in the fourth century BCE. After the battle of Pydna (168 BCE) the Romans took possession of the city, and made it the capital of Macedonia prima, the first of the four administrative districts of the Roman Macedonian Province. The four districts were later broken up, as the system was deemed over organized and inefficient.

Under Roman rule during the time of Paul, it was a largely independent city and emerged as the home of the Roman governor of all Macedonia. It was located on the important Egnatian roadway some 53 km. southwest of Philippi (between Philippi and Thessalonica). That road connected the Adriatic passage to Italy to the Hellespont and Asia.

Though not the first of the cities in the region to receive the Christian message, the city became the seat of the Bishop during the Byzantine times. This fact is attested in both the literature of the period before 692 CE and the archaeological evidence of four Christian basilicas found at the site. The proximity to the Pangean mines meant that Amphipolis became a trading center for silver and gold, but also had access to fine wool trades. The land itself was rich and produced oil and wine and wood.

Antioch (Syrian)- Antakya

Acts 6:5; 11:19-30; 12:25; 13:1-4; 14:26; 15:25-41; 18:22-23

After the death of Alexander the Great, this city was founded by Seleucus I Nicator in about 300 BCE. Choosing a site fifteen miles inland on the Orontes River, Seleucus named the site after a family name, passed from his father to his son. The site was designed to be serviced by a nearby port at the river's mouth, and is located where the Taurus and Lebanon mountains converge. The historian Strabo (contemporary of Paul) mentions that the city was about the same size as Alexandria, or slightly smaller. Diodorus of Sicily states that number to be near 300,000 freedmen. This important crossroad city had grown in both size and importance, and was the capitol of the Roman province of Syria by time of Paul.

Josephus says that Antioch was considered the third most important city of the Empire, after Rome and Alexandria (Wars 3:2.4). He also comments on a large Jewish community that lived there and converted many Greeks to proselytes of Judaism (War 7:3.3). The combination of Sea trade and desert trade on a constant east west flow, along with the political power seat placed there made the city's growth unrestrained. To the east, the Euphrates basin lead to the Parthian Empire with its coveted spice trades. To the south, the Via Maris passed through Judea to Egypt. The luxury of the city gave rise to its reputation as morally lax, and it was later chastised by the Roman satirical poet Juvenal (C2 CE) thus: "Obscene Orontes, diving underground conveys the his wealth to Tiber's hungry shores and fattens Italy with foreign whores!"

The years leading up to the visit by Paul were preceded by two significant earthquakes, and some speculate this may have made people more receptive to the message of Paul. During the reign of Caligula (37-41 CE) and then Claudius (41-54 CE) the disastrous destruction caused the city to be rebuilt, and perhaps to be more open to spiritual warnings.

In the New Testament, Antioch was one of the most prominent cities in the movement of early followers of Jesus. Some were no doubt converted at Pentecost, like Nicolas of Antioch (Acts 6:5) who was appointed to aid the church in Jerusalem. Many, however were likely first acquainted with the faith through those who fled persecution after the stoning of Stephen (Acts 11:19). Upon hearing of the growing community of faith in Antioch, Barnabas was dispatched from Jerusalem to check out the new community forming there (Acts 11:23ff). This mission was the catalyst for Barnabas to search out Saul of Tarsus, and enlist his aid in accompanying him on this mission. Paul followed Barnabas and stayed on at Antioch to preach the Gospel for the next year.

The first group of believers called by their Greek term "Christians" was at Antioch (Acts 11:26). This was the sending church for Paul and Barnabas's Mission Journeys to Asia Minor, Macedonia and Achaia (Acts 13:2; 14:26; 15:25). This church felt the brunt of the dispute over Gentile born converts to Christianity that was resolved in the Jerusalem Council (Gal. 2:11-21; Acts 15).

Antioch (Pisidian) – Yalvac

(Acts 13:13-53; 16:6; 18:23; 2 Tim. 3:11-17)

Later in the life of Seleucus Nicator I, the successor of Alexander the Great that organized Asia Minor, the city of Antioch of Pisidia was founded. He located the city strategically one hundred miles north of Perga, long after (25 years) the founding of such cities as Antioch on the Orontes and the nearby port of Seleucia. Part of the so called "lake district" of southwest Asia Minor, the strategic value of Pisidian Antioch was the guard like position it held at 3500 feet above sea level in the Taurus Mountains.

The position guarded the road access from the south, as well as the so-called "high road" from Ephesus to Syria. It was settled and maintained as the military command center of southern Galatia, and was located in the proximity of the border of Pisidia and Phrygia. Because it was near the border, the historian Strabo referred to the place as "near" Pisidia. The city was set atop a precipice described by Sir William Ramsey on his visit at the beginning of the twentieth century as "an oblong plateau varying from 50 feet to 200 feet above the plain...nearly two miles in circumference..."

By 25 BCE the city had become a colony of Rome. Westerners had poured into the city, retired soldiers with a military pension, merchants and those seeking a quieter life than those close to Rome. The expatriate Romans enjoyed full citizenship, something not attained for their indigenous counterparts until later, yet the whole city flourished and enjoyed peace and prosperity in the generation leading up to Paul and Barnabas' visit. The frequent host of Roman governors on travels from west to east, the city hosted festivals and games, and the money attracted greater investment in this, a center of Galatian activity.

On the First Mission Journey, Paul and Barnabas left the area of Perga without John Mark and proceeded to Antioch, where they entered the synagogue on the Sabbath. The address given there caused the reaction that later characterized Paul's mission journeys, some had a revival, others a riot! Driven from the city, Paul and Barnabas moved on to Iconium, experiencing an early moment of joy in the journey. It was here that Paul was moved by the hardness of his fellow countrymen and "turned to the Gentiles", a decision that would mark a concern of the Jerusalem Church for years to come.

Today, modern Yalvac is settled by a large agricultural and rural settlement amidst the still rich and fertile plains and pasturelands.

Antipatris

Acts 23:31; Joshua 12:18

Antipatris is only mentioned one time in the Book of Acts. The city had a garrison or stronghold used by Paul and Roman soldiers sent by Claudius Lysias (commander of the Roman forces at the Antonia Fortress in Jerusalem) to escorted Paul to the Roman Governor Antonius Felix at Caesarea.

Antipatris was built by Herod the Great in 9 BCE on the site of Biblical "Aphek". He named the city after his father Antipater who was the procurator of Judea in the time of Julius Caesar. The ruins of this city are now known as "Ras el-Ain". The Biblical city of Aphek was a Canaanite royal city (Joshua 12:18).

Antipatris was near the main Roman military road between Jerusalem and Caesarea, about 39 miles northwest of Jerusalem and 25 miles south of Caesarea (the capital of Judea in that period). A spring marks the site and is part of the modern name (*ain* means spring). The longest watercourse (*wadi* or dry river-bed) west of the Jordan River is Wadi Auja, which at one time carried the free flow of this spring. The road continued south from Antipatris to Lydda (present day Lod near the Ben Gurion airport) with a branch road southwest to Joppa (now "Jaffa" on the coast). There was an eastern road from the valley of Aijalon that turned south to Jerusalem. The city probably marked the northwest limit of the Roman Judean Province.

Paul and the Roman guards spent the night on their way to Caesarea. Paul was taken by the chief captain (Lysias) and sent to the Roman governor after being mobbed by a crowd on the Temple compound. After Paul's nephew related to the Roman captain that several men plotted to kill Paul, Lysias sent him away to Felix for his case to be heard in a less extreme environment (Acts 23:14-24). On the way they stopped at Antipatris, which apparently included a military post. A generation later, Antipatris was the first city Vespasian captured after he moved out of Caesarea on their way to working to conquer Jerusalem in the first revolt (67-73 CE).

Apollonia

Acts 17:1

Paul and Silas passed through the small village of Apollonia on their way to Thessalonica, and may have lodged there. There is no evidence from Scripture that they preached or ministered there, as they seemed intent on moving directly to Thessalonica. The village of Apollonia in Macedonia was located along the Via Egnatia some thirty miles west (44 km.) of Amphipolis between the Strymon and the Axius (Vardar) Rivers. The village is recalled in a modern city by the same name today, though archaeologists doubt the location is exact. The wooded region is beautiful, filled with a variety of lakes and riverbeds, an ideal place to restock supplies on a journey.

The name Apollonia was used of many ancient cities and villages. Apollonia of Illyria was perhaps the best known at that time, but not a city visited by Paul and Silas on the recorded journeys in Acts.

Appii forum

Acts 28:15

Only mentioned once in the Bible, fellow believers from Rome met Paul here, when they heard he was coming to their city. It is thought he possibly took a barge from Puteoli via the Pontine Marshes or perhaps traveled to Capua and then took the Appian Way to the Forum. This market town in Latium was located approximately 43 miles from Rome along the Appian Way. The name for the forum is translated as "market place of Appius", and is derived from the name of its founder, Appius Claudius Caecus. He not only planned the first section of the Appian Way from Rome to Capua in 312 BCE, but also built the foundation to the market at the Appii Forum.

The Roman Forum near where the Arch of Titus now stands had altars and temples (like those of the temple of the gods Castor and Pollux - Acts 28:11). Roman life was filled with celebration since in the C1 CE. A full 159 days each year were holidays (though not all celebrated) and much entertainment was provided in the circuses, theaters and other locations. Something similar may have been available in the Appii Forum, a bustling commercial center, with facilities for enjoying life and temples for worshiping deities.

The Via Appia (or Appian Way) was built about 312 BCE and went from Rome to Capua. Later the roadway was expanded (244 BCE) and connected Capua to Brundisium, approximately 350 miles from Rome. From Brundisium, travelers moving east could cross the Adriatic to Dyrrachium and continue through Macedonia to Philippi along the Egnatian Way. Several sections of the Appian Way set by the ancient Romans have been used even in modern times.

Arabia (Region)

The region of Arabia as used in the New Testament (cp. Gal. 1:17) was not the vast Arabian peninsula of today, but rather the area directly to the east and south of Provincia Judaea (in Israel and the surrounding territory). The area of Transjordan (currently the Hashemite Kingdom of Jordan), including the regions south of it, was part of the designation "Arabia".

Likely sites for Paul's journey into Arabia include cities like Petra, the Nabatean capital city. The Nabateans had expanded control over the deserts south of Damascus by the time of Paul's sojourn, operating trade routes across what is today's Israeli Negev region. In fact, the first references to the land of "Palestine" are actually references, not to the Judean cities, but to the so called Arab trade routes to the south of Judea.

The gospel made its way into this region, probably by means of some converts of the Pentecost experience (Acts 2:11), though no Epistles are singly designated to this group, and there are only scant early references to any early churches in the area. The number of Byzantine churches in the area demonstrates that the growth of the Christian message did eventually impact the region.

A second reference to Arabia in the New Testament occurs in Galatians 4:25 in relation to Sinai. This general reference shows that the Roman use of the term was much closer to the Gulf of Eilat or Aqaba than generally used today.

Assos - (Behramkale)

Acts 20:13-14

This seaport is located on the southern Troad, opposite the Island of Lesbos (due south) is located near Cape Lectum. The position of the harbor made it less susceptible to the *northerlies*, a constant wind that made navigation difficult at certain times of the year. The harbor was engineered and is not a natural one, according to a reference from the historian Strabo (Geography 13.1.57). Established about 1000 BCE by Aeolians from nearby Mitylene, the city passed through history with the succession of rulers of the Lydians, Persians, Pergamenes, and Romans.

The city, which has impressive remains, was built in the C4BCE by Hermias the "Philosopher King" on a mound of rock over 700 feet high, carefully surrounded by a wall. A student of Plato, Hermias tried to live according to the lessons he had learned by his tutor. Aristotle taught here for several years, and married an adopted daughter of King Hermias.

The ruins today stand as a marker for that C4 BCE city. Excavations have uncovered a temple to Athena that appears to have been built about 520 BCE. The interesting structure combines Doric and Ionic elements but sadly has been dismantled and shipped to museums in Paris, Boston and Istanbul. The agora, gymnasium, several baths, and a theatre complex resemble the organization of Pergamum.

In the New Testament Paul left by boat and sailed to across to Mitylene on Lesbos Island (Acts 20:14) before eventually giving his great address at Miletus to the Ephesian elders (Acts 20:15-38).

Athens

Acts 17:15-34

Paul's visit to the historic and adorned city of Athens marks one of the most challenging parts of his career as a missionary and Apostle. He arrived alone, with Silas and Timothy still in Macedonia. Though modern visitors are impressed today with the great buildings of the Acropolis and Olympian Zeus, the agora and the impressive stoas, Paul was stirred with the idolatry of the city. The history of this important center of philosophy and pagan practice extends back millenia.

Neolithic remains (4000 BCE) have been found showing that the area was inhabited well before the 6th century BCE. The name Athens is plural because it takes in the territory of a number of smaller villages, and the name stems from the goddess Athena. The focal point of the city is the naturally raised platform Acropolis. In the early stages of development, while other parts of the ancient Greek world rose to spectacular levels of civilization, Athens was just one of the city-states.

Around 620 BCE, an Athenian aristocrat Draco initiated the first steps towards order. His reputation for strictness comes down to us in the use of the term "draconian" (to indicate severe measures). The legal form was further developed by another Athenian named Solon who brought about constitutional reform as he allowed free elections that involved all social classes, except slaves, in the process of government.

After a period of tyrant rulers (Peisistratos and Sons), Athens grew steadily greater, its independence threatened only by the Persian King Darius in 490 BCE when they were defeated at Marathon, and again by his son Xerxes (the King Ahasuerus of Esther 1-2) in 480 - 479 BCE when Athenians were forced to flee from their city before beating the Persians decisively at sea at Salamis (an island near Piraeus). Despite the Athenians' victory, the temples and monuments on the Acropolis were destroyed by the Persians. Under the ruler Pericles (called the "Golden age" of Athens) the Parthenon and later the Propylaea and the Erectheion were built. With the Salamis victory, Athens became the leading naval power of the day, along with becoming the bastion of democracy and the center of cultural and intellectual activity. This age saw such great minds as Herodotus, the first Greek historian, Thucydides, who recorded the events of the Peloponnesian War, and the great classical dramatists, Aeschylus, Sophocles and Euripides, whose works were performed in the Theater of Dionysus at the southern foot of the Acropolis.

The greatness of the Athenian Empire was jealously watched by the Spartans, and in 431 BCE, the Peloponnesian War began. It was to last for thirty years, during which time Greece relapsed into chaos with the collapse of Athens. Tyranny and political corruption set in - humorously recorded during this period in the comedies of Aristophanes.

From 370 onwards, Athens began to make a recovery and soon regained both its naval power and cultural, intellectual reputation with such brilliant minds as Plato and Xenophon. Macedonia then became a political force under Philip II and Athens was specially regarded by Alexander, whose Macedonian tutor, Aristotle taught at the Lyceum in the city. The city came under the rising power of Macedonia, and its citizens joined in the conquests of Alexander the Great.

In 146 BCE, Athens fell under the rule of the rising western power of the Romans who remained its master for over 500 years. The city flourished under their patronage of some of the Emperors (Hadrian), but suffered looting of others (Nero). It was fashionable in the earlier Roman world to be educated in Athens (Cicero and Horace) but by 529 C.E. the Christian Roman Emperor Justinian decreed the schools of philosophy to be closed. The emergence of Christianity caused the downfall of the city, although ironically, Greek was the language of the new religion.

The concept of tourism also emerged during this period. Wealthy Romans were keen travellers who loved the ancient classical world which they emulated. They traveled widely in Greece, reserving the best of their attention for Athens. A thriving trade in antiques and works of art also developed since they were eagerly sought after by the Romans for the decoration of their villas.

Under **Byzantine** domination, Athens diminished in importance. After the fall of Contantinople to the Crusaders in 1204, Athens fell to Boniface III Marquis of Monferrat as his share of the old Byzantine Empire. The power of Frankish Greece was eventually destroyed by the Catalans of Spain around 1311. After the rule of the Sicilians came the Venetians, then came four centuries of occupation by the Turks from 1462.

In 1834, Athens became the capital of liberated Greece. During World War I, the city was occupied by British and French troops, while in World War II, suffered under German occupation. The modern city was designed and constructed by Bavarian architects, since the first King of Greece was the Bavarian Prince Otto.

The **Plaka**, near the Acropolis was designated to be the old Athens, and it survives with all the character, interest and wonder that its long history attaches to it.

The **Agora** was the central meeting place of ancient Athens. It was both the market place and the heart of Athenian daily life. The **Stoa of Attalos**, King of Pergamum, was built as a trading center in 159 BCE It was reconstructed by the American School of Classical Studies and houses finds from excavation in the area. To the east is the area of the Roman Forum, begun in the reign of Julius Caesar and completed under Hadrian.

The **Plaka** today consists of a mixture of ancient Greek and Roman ruins, Byzantine churches, Turkish mosques and nineteenth centrury houses.

The Athenian **Acropolis** stands alone in its unique combination of grandeur, beauty and historical associations. In Classical times the Pantheanic Way ended in a ramp straight up, but the modern approach is different. The **Propylae**, a monumental gateway designed by Mnesicles to replace an earlier entrance, its axis aligned to that of the Parthenon. It provides the only example, before Hellenistic times, of designing one building in direct relationship to another. Built of Pentelic marble, it remained intact till the 13th century, after which the Franks and Turks, as well as lightning strikes and war damaged it and altered it proportions. The Temple of **Athena Nike** was built in 427 BCE to commemorate the victory of the Athenians over the Persians. The **Parthenon** represents the culmination of the Doric style of architecture. It was erected in 447 - 438 as the cardinal feature of Pericles plan. Ictinus was the architect an Pheidias supervised the whole of the sculptures. In the sixth century BCE, it was converted to a Christian Church. Under Justianian, dedicated to Saint Sophia (the Holy Wisdom), then to the Virgin Mother of God (Theotokos). Then as a cathedral of the Frankish dukes it followed the Latin rite. During the Ottoman occupation it became a mosque and was destroyed by the Venetians in the seventeenth century. The **Erechteion** is the most original specimen of Greek architecture. A joint shrine of Athena and Poseidon Erechteus was finished after 395 BCE, and owes its curious plan to the sacrosanct nature of the sanctuaries that preceded it. Like the Parthenon it became known by a name that originally applied only to one of its parts.

The **Kerameikos** includes the ruins of the Dipylon and Sacred Gates. Here roads from Eleusis, Piraeus and Boetia converged upon that from the Academy (Plato's Academy), so that by this way most ancient travellers entered the city.

Cemeteries existed in this area from the 12th century BCE By the 7th century the inner area becomes a quarter of potters and smiths and the outer, which is the cemetery, is separated by the city wall. The Academy road outside the Gate becomes the Demosion Sema, the cemetery reserved for state tombs and cenotaps. It is here that Pericles delivered the famous oration (Thycydides).

The work of Paul in Athens left its mark, with a few converts including Damaris and Dionysus the Areopagite. In the succeeding generations several important Christian thinkers rose from the Athenian Church.

Attalia- Antalya

Acts 14:25-28

Not to be confused with Attalia in Lydia, this city near the mouth of the Cataractes River (modern Aksu) was the chief port of

Pamphylia. After a temporary peace was established in 188 BCE at Apameia, western Pamphylia came under the control of Pergamon. Because the port at Side was still outside the boundary of his Kingdom, Attalus II King of Pergamon (159-138 BCE) founded the new Mediterranean port at Attalia (and apparently named it after himself). Upon his death it was passed to his son Attalus III, who willed to Rome when he died. The Roman grip on the city was from time to time challenged by Pirates.

The city today bears the ruins of antiquity in a modest museum. A tower over the harbor (Hidirlik Kulesi) bears evidence of a lighthouse that existed on that location since the C2 CE, probably built over the mausoleum of a hero that stood at the time of Paul's visit. Also from that century is the three-arched Hadrianic gate built about 135 CE. The city became the seat of the Bishop from the rise of Christianity in the Empire until 1084, when the city was elevated again to the seat of the Archbishopric. It has Ottoman period walls, and two prominent mosques: the C16th CE Murat Pasa Mosque and the C18th CE Tekeli Mehmet Pasa Mosque.

Berea

Acts 17:10,13; 20:4

The city of Berea (modern Veria) was founded in the Archaic Period in the southwestern part of Macedonia, some 73 km west of Thessalonica. Ruins extend to 700 BCE (though scarce), when the city probably began as an agricultural market center. The founders were no doubt Thracians and Phrygians driven out by the "Makadne" in one of the archaic transitions. The mythological beginning of the city is ascribed to a daughter of Ocean, the Titan that married Thetys (another Titan) and bore the "Oceanids" (Nymphs of the great rivers). The myth probably recalls the main reason the city was founded on this location. The city is set on a ridge with the well watered nearby basins of the Eliakomon and Axios Rivers. The alluvial plains north of Mount Vermio were (and still are) still rich in apple, peach and pear orchards. Scholars believe the city may have reached 60,000 to 70,000 people at its zenith (about twice its modern population), but this is speculation. A major electric dam on the

Eliakomon River today provides industrial sector work today, and the area is still considered reasonably wealthy.

Extensive excavations have not been attempted in the area. The major artifacts in the local museum, though quite interesting, are mainly funerary monuments. A few sections of the ancient city wall are displayed on the edges of the city. With few physical finds, scholars are left to seek information from ancient historians. Thucydides (the Classical period general that was expelled from Athens after losing to the Persians) referred to the place. The city opened their gates to Rome after the Battle of Pydna (168 BCE) and was taken by the Romans without resistance. Under the Roman administration, the city became well populated, partly due to the extension of the Egnatian Way through the region of Berea to its north.

Long after Paul's preaching the Christian community thrived in the city. One tradition says that Sopater, son of Pyrrhus, was the first convert of the Berean church (mentioned in Acts 20:4). The other (better established) tradition is that of the "Synaxar" (Orthodox Calendar of the Saints) that refers to Karpus (one of the 70 Disciples) as first Bishop of the city. Much later, the Middle Ages brought great prosperity to the region. Indeed, the city was considered one of the most important in the region, with several beautiful churches including frescoes as old as the C12 CE. More than 37 churches of the period have been identified, but scholars believe more than 100 churches existed in the period!

Paul fled in the night from Thessalonica to Berea (Acts 17:10) and taught in the synagogue there (during the Second Mission Journey). In the synagogue he found people who were eager to receive the Gospel and compare it with the Hebrew Scriptures. The Berean search of the Scriptures daily became an example to early Christians, and the name was carried to later churches everywhere. Luke notes that many believed, and includes that "honorable women which were Greeks, and of men, not a few" (Acts 17:12) came to Jesus. The reception was probably a true respite to the Apostle and his team, but it was short-lived. Jews that did not believe the message of Jesus preached by Paul came from Thessalonica when they learned Paul continued ministry there. They came and stirred up the people against

Paul, causing him to once again flee, this time to Athens. Paul left Silas and Timothy to care for the believers in Berea and in Thessalonica for a short while.

In the modern city stands a "Triptych monument" stands in reminder of Paul's work. The monument includes three steps that were removed from a salvage dig at a nearby school property. The steps were reputed to have been from the location of the ancient synagogue. The display is made of colorful mosaic tile and displays three panels: 1) The Macedonian man vision, 2) Paul, 3) The address to the Bereans.

Bithynia (Region)

The geographical region on the southern edge of the Black Sea, and east of the Bosphorus and Sea of Marmara were the Roman province of Bithynia. Settled in the Dark Ages, the region was generally brought under the legendary Sardian King Croessus (C6 BCE). A Bithynian ruler of the C3 BCE allowed the passage and settlement of Gauls into the region, forming the territory of "Galatia" immediately south of Bithynia. The territory was transferred to the Romans in 74 BCE, ad linked in administration to Pontus (as one territory). Today it is the northern portion of the Republic of Turkey.

Paul desired to travel the routes east of Troas toward the Eastern Black Sea via Bithynia and Pontus, but was directed by the Spirit to Macedonia, along the Via Egnatia road (cp. Acts 16:6-10). Apparently there were early followers of Jesus in the region (cp. 1 Pet. 1:1) and the Apostles certainly considered this area important for evangelism and outreach of the Christian message. By 111 CE there was a well-established Christian presence, and Pliny the Younger complained of the Christians on letters to Emperor Trajan, because the Christians opposed some of Pliny's directives.

Caesarea

Acts 8:40; Acts 9:30; Acts 10:1, 24; 11: 11; 12:19; Acts 18:22; 21:8,9,16; Acts 21:7-40; Acts 23:23,33; Acts 24, 25, 26; Acts 25:1,4,6,13, 23; Acts 25:11; 26: 1-13

For more than 600 years the capital city of the Roman Province of Judea was the port city of Caesarea. It was a critical economic seaport during the time of Jesus and the Apostles, located on the beach between what is now called Tel Aviv and Haifa, about 23 miles south of Mount Carmel. A journey from Jerusalem (as Paul traveled with his Roman escorts) was 64 miles.

The city was constructed by Herod the Great who sought favor with the Romans (while balancing his relationship with his constituent Jews). He knew there was no excellent Mediterranean port east of Pireaus in Athens, and chose the site of Caesarea (named in honor of his patron Caesar Augustus). He chose the site of a military garrison called "Strato's tower" and built the port using the most modern techniques available. Some scholars believe the first use of underwater concrete was at the port works. The city also acted as a Roman garrison and took twelve years to build.

Herod spared nothing to make this city a lavish Roman city. It featured a magnificent hippodrome, an amphitheater, a dramatic theatre (where the remains of a dedication stone has been found inscribed with the name of Pontius Pilate), a seaside palace and many ornate public buildings. It also boasted of an Imperial temple (probably in honor of Augustus Caesar) and an aqueduct for a consistent water supply from Mt. Carmel's foothills. The garrison numbered as much as three thousand Roman troops during the period and was manned (in part) by the Italian band (Acts 10:1).

The harbor engineering displayed Roman genius. A twenty-two foot wide breakwater was built against the gales in the south. The base was filled with gigantic blocks of limestone and fill cement. Some pier columns measured 50 x 18 x 9 feet, and several are still visible today (extending 150 feet from the shore).

This city was the center of Roman government for hundreds of years and the residence of the Governor of Judea. Pontius Pilate lived there during his near ten-year tenure in office. At times it experienced disturbances because of the mix of Jews and Romans, Caesarea was a strong economic and Roman military presence. When the Jews rebelled in 66 CE many Jews in the city were massacred. King Herod Agrippa II and Bernice his consort found refuge here when the war broke out.

Luke includes a number of events at Caesarea in the Book of Acts. Philip the evangelist preached and lived there with his four prophetess daughters (Acts 8:40; 21:8,9). After Paul's conversion, the brethren helped Paul escape trouble and took him to the port of Caesarea to locate a ship bound for Tarsus (his hometown - Acts 9:30). Peter first preached to a Gentile, the Roman centurion named Cornelius in this city. This was the first city where the gospel was preached to a non-Jew. This caused tension in the Jewish minds of Peter and the other Apostles.

Caesarea was a port call for Paul on his missionary journeys (Acts 18:22). Paul later stopped in Caesarea on his way to Jerusalem and stayed with Philip and his daughters (Acts 21:8). It was during this stay that the prophet Agabus warned him of trouble if he continued on his journey to Jerusalem. Much later, the Apostle Paul was sent to Felix governor of Judea. On his arrival to Caesarea, he appeared before Felix (Acts 24) and was imprisoned for two years waiting to make his defense. Festus, the successor to Felix gave him audience, as did King Herod Agrippa II.

There were other cities that bore the name "Caesarea". One such city known as Caesarea Philippi was in the jurisdiction of Agrippa fifty miles from Damascus on the southern slopes of Mount Hermon. Near Caesarea Philippi Jesus gave important teaching to His Disciples (Matthew 16:13-20, Mark 8:28ff).

Cenchrea

Acts 18:18; Romans 16:1

Paul and his companions visited Cenchrea after nearly eighteen months of ministry in Corinth, during the Second Mission

Journey. The city was a small port located more than two miles south of Isthmia and about six miles east of Corinth. It was constructed along the road from Isthmia that leads south to the so-called "Baths of Helen" of antiquity. Cenchrea functioned as the eastern harbor of the Corinthians for shipping on the Saronic Gulf. Corinth also had another port, Lechaeum, to the west of Corinth on the Corinthian Gulf. Ships were safely guided between the two harbors to avoid the danger of sailing around Cape Malea. As a town frequented by seafarers, Cenchrea was also a sacred town to Poseidon.

Excavations were begun in 1963 by the American School, University of Chicago and Indiana University under the auspices of Professors Scranton and Ramage. The city had not been excavated because it had been a military area until that time. Though extensive excavations still need to be carried on at the site, the port was positively identified by coinage. The coinage depicts the harbor as surrounded by porticoes with a significant storage capacity. Above the site was a Roman period Temple thought to be of Tyche (fortune). On the wide pier that stretched about five hundred feet into the sea, a Temple of Isis and a *piscinae* (fish tank) were located. Further away, about half a mile from the harbor was the monument for a "Tomb of Regulus", the chief patron of the city and first president of the Isthmian games. The tomb was about 20 years old when Paul visited here.

The port has some important New Testament connections, as it was the site of Paul's completion of a vow, as well as the home of Phoebe (Rom. 16:1,2). Since vows among Jews were often completed with a shaving of the head, it appears that Paul had completed a private vow. Some scholars believe the vow was to remain in Corinth (despite the pagan and degraded surroundings) until God indicated that he should leave.

Excavations also reveal a thriving Byzantine presence. A complex of that period was located including at least two churches. The site appears to have been completely destroyed by two devastating earthquakes, in 365 CE and 375 CE. A small dock and a partially submerged Basilica are all that are easily seen today, though other remains are exposed in bulks on the hill just north of the harbor area.

Chios (Island of)

Acts 20:15

The island of Chios (in the Aegean Sea) is only five miles (8 km.) off the western Turkish coast south of the island of Lesbos. The island measures near thirty kilometers in length (north to south), and varies between ten and twenty kilometers in width. It is about twelve miles west of Smyrna across the narrow channel. Formed by volcanic flow, the highest point in the island is in the north at Mt. Pelineo (ASL +1297 meters; 4255 feet). The island is well watered, with sufficient winter rains to produce the celebrated harvests of citrus fruit, mulberries, grapes, cotton, tobacco, vegetables and lentisk (also called mastic tree). The lentisk is used in the production of the alcoholic "mastika", and is the base of a resin used in chewing gum, cakes, oriental syrups and deserts.

The island was settled by Ionians in antiquity, and field excavation has yielded evidence of some settlement activity extending to the C19th BCE. In C8th BCE, the island joined the Ionian confederacy (with Samos and several Asia Minor cities). By the C6th BCE, the island enjoyed prosperity and was the first to engage in the slave trade. The Persian onslaught of 493 BCE ended the prosperity, and the island periodically changed "masters" from Athens to Macedonia and eventually to Rome.

Though under Roman government, the port was quite independent for much of the Roman period. Paul sailed by Chios on his way to address the Ephesian elders Miletus (and eventually Jerusalem for the beginning of Pentecost - Acts 20:15). This reference to the journey should probably be translated "along the channel of Chios" rather than "against Chios". This particular journey included stops where he strengthened, instructed and warned the believers in different places as well as bidding them farewell, sensing that he would not see them again (cp. 20: 25).

Chios lost many inhabitants during the Early Byzantine period, as pirates ran much of the legitimate trade of the eastern Aegean away. The once prosperous island farms broke down until the Byzantine rulers discovered its value in agriculture.

Eventually the island revived. It became a holding of the Venetians by 1172 CE and a centerpiece of the maritime "empire" of the Genoese from 1346 to 1566.

Cilicia

Tucked at the northeastern corner of the Mediterranean (southeastern Asia Minor), the region of Cilicia was a small plain (30-60 miles wide and 300 miles long) bordered by mountains to the north and east, and the sea to the south. The western part of Cilicia, called Tracheia (or "the rugged place"), was an extended plateau of the uplifted Taurus Mountain range. The eastern part (called Cilicia Pedias or "the plain of Cilicia") stretched as a fertile plain between the Taurus Mountains to the north, and Mount Amanus to the south.

The western part of Cilicia was associated with the dens of pirates. This difficult territory has a history rife with tales of treasures and villains. The eastern plain had sixteen cities that remained proud and semi-autonomous even under Rome. A main prosperous university city of Tarsus stood out among them. A significant roadway lead through Cilicia's main pass called the "Cilician Gates" to the inland beyond the Taurus Mountain wall and on to Cappadocia.

Cilicia was presumable a settlement originated by the Hittite Kingdom, with some Syrian and Phoenician settlers. Much later it was part of the sweeping acquisition of the armies of Alexander the Great. The Seleucid ruler Antiochus IV (Epiphanes) is credited with granting the city of Tarsus a "free city state" status, and settling Jews in the area to stimulate business (in exchange for making them free citizens –171 BCE).

Though it officially became a Roman province before 100 BCE, it was not properly controlled until General Pompey drove out the pirates and controlled the southern Asia Minor coast in 67 BCE. About 55 years before Paul's birth in Tarsus, Cicero was governor of the region (51 BCE). Augustus neglected the direct control, and allowed other Kingdoms of Asia Minor to rule as client kingdoms over the western area, and Syria to exercise control in the eastern plain. The linkage to Syria is understood in the New Testament, where Syria is mentioned together with

Cilicia (Gal. 1:21 in variant texts; Acts 15:23, 41). The gospel reached the area early (Acts 15:23). The northeastern part of the Mediterranean was referred to in Acts as the "sea of Cilicia" (Acts 27:5).

Clauda (Island of)

Acts 27:16

Clauda (also Cauda, modern Gavdos) was an island located 40 kilometers due south of the southern coast of Crete. The island was not visited by Paul, but was mentioned as a navigation note by Luke as the ship they were on was pushed steadily off course in the Mediterranean journey to Rome. A tempestuous wind called the *euroclydon* drove the ship past Clauda. The crew used the small island to block some of the fierce winds, and under girded the boat with lashes. Following the sighting of Clauda, they were driven by the storm for many days without seeing sun, stars or land. Paul encouraged the crew and passengers and told them they would not perish. The end of the storm pushed them to the island called Melita (Acts 27:16-28:1).

Cnidus

Acts 27:7

Positioned on a peninsula that projected as an obstacle from the coastline between Cos and Rhodes, the port of Cnidus helped service the maritime traffic of southwest Asia Minor in antiquity. The peninsula was known in antiquity for the defeat of the Spartan navy in 394 BCE at the hands of the Athenian admiral Conon (commanding a Persian fleet). The city is mentioned in 1 Maccabees 15:23 as having a Jewish population, and was a free city. Paul's struggling boat from Alexandria, Egypt (he was under custody and bound for Rome) came "over against Cnidus" in the journey.

Colosse (or Colossae)

(Epistle to the Colossians, Philemon 10,23)

Along a main inland road from Ephesus to the Euphrates River, Colossae shared the beauty of the Lycus Valley with its sister cities: Hierapolis (12 miles northwest) and Laodicea (12 miles west). The original roads from Ephesus and Sardis joined there, and this defensible and well-watered hill became a strategic point in antiquity. Declining in importance by the time of Paul's Epistle to them, they had already been surpassed in size by the other Lycus Valley cities. Strabo lists Colossae with smaller villages, not with major cities. The city received an Epistle because of the unique and insidious errors taking hold there, not because of its size. The site is abandoned today, near the village of Honaz.

By the C5BCE, Herodotus noted the "large city of Phrygia". The center of a large and prosperous textile and wool industry, Xenophon remarked this was "a well populated city, large and wealthy". The dark red wool from the region took the special name *colossinium*. The attraction of wealth and industry brought together a mix of Jews, Phrygians, and Greek traders. This combination no doubt helps the modern reader of Colossians account for the variety of philosophies addressed in the corrective Epistle.

The gospel probably arrived in Colossae with Paul's preaching in Ephesus (cp. Acts 19:10) on the Third Mission Journey. Perhaps Epaphras, the Lycus Valley's own evangelist heard Paul at Ephesus and returned with the message. It is impossible to know for sure, but it seems as though Paul had not yet visited at the time of the writing of the Epistle to the Colossians. Philemon and his slave Onesimus apparently were both natives of Colossae. The omission of any reference by Paul to the great earthquake of 60 CE causes many scholars to believe Paul had not yet heard the news, or the Epistle predates the quake (Tacitus records the quake, Annals 14.27). Epaphras visited Paul during his house arrest, and brought news of the Lycus Valley to Paul, refreshing him during the imprisonment.

Coos (Island of)

Acts 21:1

Coos is long and narrow, the second largest island of the Dodecanese (behind Rhodes). The island is not far from the shore of Asia Minor (near Halicanarssus), and is most noted as the ancient home of Hippocrates the physician. The island has a long and colorful history.

Some time in the Greek Dark Ages (1150-800 BCE) the Achaeans arrived (after the decline of Minoan Crete). By the 11th century BCE the Dorians invaded Kos and expelled the Achaeans. In the Archaic Period (800-500 BCE) the islands of Kos, Nisyros, Karpathos, and Kalymnos played an important part in the Trojan War according to The Odyssey. After the fall of Troy, local Greek mythology presents: "Podarios, son of the god Asklepios (the Doctor from Thessaly) settled on the island after a shipwreck. From this time, the family of the Asklepidai lived on the island (Hippocrates was introduced as the 18th descendant).

In the 7th century BCE, Kos joined a federation with six other cities in Asia Minor, Rhodes, Kalymnos and Nisyros. Later during the Classical Period (500-336 BCE), the island of Kos (as the other cities of Asia Minor) was subdued by the Persians. In 479 BCE the island was represented at the battle of Salamina (where Xerxes was defeated). During the Peloponnesian war (431-404 B.C.E.) Kos allied with Athens. For this the island paid a high tribute when the Spartan Commander Astochos invaded the island in 411 BCE. In 394, after a brief treaty with Sparta, the Koans once again allied with Athens. Under the influence of Athens democracy was introduced. Life on Kos was stable and the island enjoyed prosperity until the invasion of King Mausolos of Halikarnasos in 358. The island recovered under Alexander and the Diadoche. In 334 BCE the island allied with Macedonian and Alexander the Great. The ports became places of supply for the advancing Greek armies.

During the Roman Period Kos became a part of the Eastern colony of the Roman Empire and was granted special privileges (from 82 BCE). Some of these were stripped away during the reign of Augustus and cause a decline that was compounded by a terrible earthquake in 27 BCE. The island recovered again, in part due to its important reputation as a healing center. In the Book of Acts, the island was an overnight stop during part of Paul's journey to Jerusalem. Paul came from Miletus, and sailed to Coos, Rhodes and Patara (Acts 21:1).

By the Byzantine Period (300-1000 CE) Kos flourished as part of the Byzantine Empire. Close to Asia Minor, the island was continuously attacked by both pirates and Turks. By the Crusader Period, (1204 C.E.) the island was occupied by the Venetians. The Ottoman Rule (1450-1830) began in 1457 CE, when a powerful Turkish army looted the island. Turks again subdued the island under Sultan Sulieman, but the Koans continued with a resistance movement. On May 5th, 1912 Italian troops invaded the island and expelled the Turks. In 1934 an earthquake destroyed 80% of the housing and monumental architecture of the island, but most was later restored. The occupation continued under the Germans in 1943 (with a short respite of 20 days when the English ruled). The 18 months of German occupation brought inhumane suffering to the Koans. In 1945 the island came under British control and was rebuilt. Finally, on March 7th, 1948 became part of modern Greece.

Corinth

Acts18: 1,27; 19:1; Romans 16:23; 1 Corinthians 1:2; 4:17; 5:9; 16:15; 2 Corinthians 1:1,23; II Timothy 4:20; I Thessalonians 3:6

Because Paul spent more than one and one half years at Corinth during his Second Mission Journey, the city remains important to students of the Book of Acts. This city was constructed in antiquity on a narrow isthmus, a cosmopolitan city that connected the Peloponnese and the Balkan Peninsula. Corinth had deep-water harbors on each side, with Cenchrea on the east end, and Lechaeum on the west. Thus the city's natural location made it a very wealthy commercial and shipping center.

The city also enjoyed a long and important history among Greek "city-states" from the Neolithic through Archaic Periods. Scholars agree that a Neolithic settlement was located near the Peirene Spring from about 4,000 BCE. That settlement eventually disappeared, but eight distinct settlements are known from the plain near Corinth by 2,000 BCE. By 1800 BCE, influence and invasion affected the development. (A Phoenician temple to Aphrodite was established.) Following the Dark Age of Greece (1100-800 BCE) with its characteristic invasion waves, the expansion of the Dorian people group is illustrated by their colonization of Syracuse and Corcyra from areas like Corinth. Some scholars claim the archaic foundations of the organized city appear to date to the C8 BCE. In the two centuries that followed (before the Classical Period) the city appropriated a number of myths that actually originated elsewhere. It adopted the Pegasus (winged horse) and the mythology of its capture by Bellerophon (a story that belonged originally to Asia Minor), and made it the symbol of Corinth.

By the Classical Period, Corinth was one of the powerhouse city-states, ranking with Sparta and Athens in value (though not as militarily strong). Corinth was essential to the routing of the Persians during the period, and played special roles in a number of campaigns. During the Peloponnesian Wars (the period of tensions between Athens and Sparta, 431-404 BCE), Corinth often found itself in a difficult position between the two cities. In general, the strategic position and economy aided the city in becoming a key player in many alliances. It was important to Philip II (who garrisoned the mount of Acrocorinth) and later even became the capital of the Aechean League for a short time before it aligned against the rising Roman power.

Because of its stance against the expansion of Roman power, the Roman General Mummius laid the city waste in 146 BCE. By 46 BCE, Julius Caesar re-colonized the area and gave it the status of Roman capital of Achaia. From that time Corinth enjoyed much freedom as an independent city.

The city had a large theater and was frequented by the Emperors of Rome for the Isthmian games. Several scholars note the population may have exceeded 400,000 for some of the Roman period. Another important attraction to the Roman city was in the Acrocorinth. This hill, about 1886 feet above the plain, formed a natural and impregnable defense for ancient Corinth. By the time of the Romans such defenses were not important, but the establishment of the great temple of Aphrodite and its numerous temple prostitutes (the number in some sources is reported at more than 1000!) made the place notable to ancient historians. The city agora or market place boasted nightclubs or bars (33 taverns have been excavated). The city was known for luxury, pleasure and especially immorality – a key to concern of Paul in his letters to the Corinthians. The city was a mixture population (Greeks, Romans, Jews, Italians, etc.) and attracted thousands by its reputation for "base" entertainment. Important trade links were maintained with Italy and Asia Minor via Ephesus.

Paul's initial visit to Corinth was on his Second Missionary Journey, when he arrived from Athens about 50-51 CE. He spent one year and six months while working as a tentmaker. He lodged with Aquila and Priscilla who moved to Corinth after the expulsion of Jews from Rome by Emperor Claudius (49 or 50 CE). Paul told Timothy and Silas to remain behind to strengthen churches when Paul was forced to leave Berea and they rejoined Paul in Corinth from Macedonia. When they arrived, Paul was busy with forming the new congregation of followers as he " reasoned in the synagogue every Sabbath, and persuaded the Jews and the Greeks." He began preaching in the Jewish community and when the leadership opposed him he departed from the synagogue and taught the disciples in the house of Justus located next to the synagogue. Among those who believed was the chief synagogue ruler, Crispus.

Paul was assured by a vision that Jesus would protect him if he remained in Corinth at the ministry task. Shortly after the vision the message was tested. He was brought to the judgment (bema) seat before Gallio (the newly appointed deputy of Achaia) by some local Jewish leaders who accused him of persuading people to worship God contrary to the law (Acts 18: 12-16). Gallio chose not to involve himself in the matter and drove them away. This judgment seat that Paul was brought before has been uncovered in the center of the market place or agora. There were two lower steps that surrounded a high platform (five feet or so), covered with marble. The platform was more than thirty feet long, and had been restored by archaeologists.

The friends Paul met at Corinth (Aquila and Priscilla) became true partners in ministry. No doubt their encouragement helped to revive the Apostle after the terrible experiences associated with his second journey as he came into Macedonia and Achaia. In addition to their encouragement, we have record of their continued ministry after they departed Corinth and went to Ephesus. A Messianic teacher named taught about Jesus to the local believers, but taught about the baptism of John. Aquila and Priscilla knew from listening to Paul the message had progressed further and took Apollos aside and explained to him the more complete information. Perhaps during those conversations Apollos gained the desire to move on to Corinth, for he continued the work that Paul had started there and was mightily used to further the ministry. (see Acts 18:23,24,26-28;19:1)

Paul's Epistle to the Romans was written in Corinth. (Romans 16:23) Paul was evidently staying with a man named Gaius (Paul's host) and aided by the amanuensis Tertius who was scribed the letter. The first and second epistles to the Thessalonians were also written from Corinth (I Thessalonians 3: 6-7). Timothy returned from Thessalonica with reports on how the ministry progressed after Paul's forced departure.

Paul wrote the first Epistle to the Corinthians from Ephesus some time later. Timothy may have been the bearer of this letter to the Corinthians (I Corinthians 4:17). In the second Epistle to them (see 2 Corinthians 7) it appears that Paul may have sent Titus with a 'painful letter' that Paul had written to the Corinthians, rebuking them for tolerating immorality in their midst. That letter is widely believed to be "lost" and not part of the record of the New Testament. It appears that Titus may have gone to Corinth with this letter or he may have gone after the letter got to the Corinthians and was able to receive from them, their earnestness to be right before God and deal with the sin issues. The second Epistle to the Corinthians (which may be actually a third letter) was written from Macedonia by Paul, which amongst other commended the Corinthians for their good response to the 'painful letter'.

Crete (Island of)

Acts 27:7,12,13,21; Titus 1:12; Deuteronomy 2:23; I Samuel 30:14; Ezekiel 25:16;Amos 9:7

Crete has an important history of about four thousand years. This large mountainous Mediterranean island at the south of the Cycladic island chain was likely the place known in the Hebrew Scriptures as "Caphtor" (Deuteronomy 2:23; Amos 9:7). The island of Crete measures about 150 miles long (west to east) and between 7 and 35 miles wide. The island has four small mountain ranges and was most fertile on the east, where the first settlements were constructed.

After the excavations by Evans at the palace in Knossos, scholars realized that the foundations of European history were partially rooted in a palace culture called the Minoan civilization (after the legendary King Minos). Archaeology of ancient Greece has yielded two distinct cultures, one associated with the mainland site at the archaic site of Mycenae (called the Mycenaean civilization) and the Minoan palace culture (found in four palace sites in Crete).
Exploration of the Minoan civilization has uncovered some truly stunning pieces of art, colorful places and intricate jewelry. The culture was well refined, with several unique bull related cultic rituals. One of the first sculptured pieces that included a man in a position that showed movement was discovered amid the ruins.

Many scholars believe the terrible devastation of the volcano at Santorini (Thira) and the subsequent Dorian invasions (a few hundred years later) from the north caused the migration of many tribes from the area. Three tribes that journeyed east included (according to this theory) the Tjekker, the Sherden and the Peleste. It is possible the Peleste was the largest tribe and the term found its way in to the Bible in the word "Philistine". The "Cherethites" that formed part of the personal guard for King David were probably descendants of Cretans from the Peleste (1 Samuel 30:14) that made their way to the coasts of Egypt and the area near Gaza about 100-150 years before.

During the Classical and Hellenistic periods, the island was primarily comprised of agricultural villages. By 100 BCE it had become a haven for pirates that periodically harassed Roman vessels. By Senate decree, Crete and Cyrene formed a Roman province by 68 BCE and a significant Jewish population was noted (they appealed to the Romans for protection). Gortys was made capital of the island by the Romans.

In the Book of Acts Cretan Jews were in Jerusalem on the day of Pentecost (Acts 2:11). Paul's first visit to Crete (much later) was on his way to Rome just before the shipwreck at the island of Melita (Acts 27:7). Paul visited Crete later (after the record of the Book of Acts) and left Titus to take care of the churches in this island (Titus 1:5).

Paul's sayings concerning the people of Crete were perhaps his least complementary of any in his writings. He declared the people as well known people of indulgence. Paul wrote to Titus using a Greek quote of the poet Epimenides (used also by Paul in Athens in Acts 17:28a): "The Cretans are alway liars, evil beasts, slow bellies" (Titus 1:12). He then called the "true". Titus was left to exhort, rebuke and bring order in the Cretan church (Titus 1:5,13; 2:15). A sixth century Byzantine church of St. Titus was erected to recall the works and struggle of this Pastor.

Cyprus (Island of)

Acts 4:36; 11:19,20; 13:4; 15:39; 21:3,16; 17:4

Departing from the Seleucian port, some 16 miles from Antioch, the team arrived by ship into the port of Salamis on the eastern side of Cyprus in an undisclosed amount of time (probably two days by sail depending on winds). After preaching in the synagogues of the city, they proceeded across the island as far as Paphos, a port on the west of the island (Acts 13:4-6).

The long island of Cyprus (225 kilometers) is the largest island of the eastern Mediterranean, situated about 100 kilometers off the Syrian coast (as well as the same distance south of the Turkish coast). Cyprus is not mentioned by name in the Hebrew Scriptures, but reference to the "Kittim" (Gen. 10) was probably the inhabitants of Kition (near modern Larnaca). By the time of

Paul's journeys, Rome was mater of the island, though it acted with much autonomy. Though Cyprus was log considered an ally of Rome, it was historically Egyptian controlled. The island became a Roman province in 58 BCE (initially as an annex of Cilicia), but in 47 BCE the island was returned to Egypt. With the suicide of Cleopatra (31 BCE), Cyprus came under direct Roman control. Later (22 BCE) Augustus proclaimed Cyprus one of the senatorial provinces under a praetorian Proconsul.

The specific route of their land journey is not specified in the text, yet there are arguments to suggest the route may be along the major Roman route of the day. First, Paul and Barnabas appear to intend to make their way in haste, and do not plan to spend an excessive amount of time in any one city. Though they had been directed by the Spirit of God and the Church at Antioch, the actual plan of the trip is undisclosed in the narrative. Second, on other journeys they took advantage of the Roman roads. Scholars suggest that Paul used the Via Sebaste to access Pisidian Antioch in the First Journey, as well as the Via Egnatia to cross from Neapolis to Berea in Macedonia in the Second Journey.

In the case of the Cyprus journey, the men had opportunity to access a roadway from the east coast of Cyprus to the west. They apparently had two choices for the journey, one following the northern coast, and one to the south. A number of scholars have accumulated careful evidence for the roads between Salamis and Paphos using traveler itineraries found in Roman record, and following the archaeological discoveries of Roman milestones. The route favored by scholars was that which headed for Citium on the south coast, westward to Amathus, continuing to Curium and terminating in Paphos. The southern journey could have been made between Sabbaths, but may have extended a day or two longer. The route no doubt took them along the path of some significant pagan centers.

Though the only cities on Cyprus mentioned in the narrative of Acts are Salamis and Paphos, Paul and Barnabas no doubt traveled by way of other cities en route. If they used the road along the south coast as suggested, they would have passed through Citium, Amathus and Curium before reaching Paphos. Amathus had been granted the status of asylum in 22 CE because of their civic sanctuaries, as had the cities of Salamis (Olympian Zeus) and Paphos (Paphian Aphrodite). Amathus boasted a sanctuary of Aphrodite.

Barnabas and John Mark returned to the island when Paul left with Silas to Asia Minor to take the message of the Jerusalem Council (Acts 15:39) but no firm knowledge of their itinerary was preserved. The mark of Barnabas on the island is unmistakable in the various traditions and local churches.

Damascus

Acts 9:2,3,8,10,19,22,24,25,27; 22:5,6,10,11; 26:12,20; II Corinthians 11:32,33; Galatians 1:17;Genesis 14:15; 15:2; II Samuel 8:5,6; II Kings 8:7; 11: 23,24; 15:18; 19:15; 20:34; 22:34; II Kings 5:12; 8:7,9; 14:28; 16:9,10,11,12; I Chronicles 18:5,6; II Chronicles 16:2; 24:23; 28:5,23; Isaiah 7:8; 8:4; 10:9; 17:1,3; Jeremiah 49:23,24,27; Ezekiel 27:18; 47:16,17,18; 48:1; Amos 1:3-5; 3:12; 5:27; Zechariah 9:1

From the time of Paul stumbled into the streets of Damascus blindly following the word of Jesus to await healing, the city was an important place in the narrative of the Book of Acts. The connection of the city to the Scripture did not begin with Paul, however. Damascus is mentioned as early in the Scriptures as the time of Abraham. This city was likely the homeland of Abraham's trusted servant Eleazar (Genesis 15:2).

Damascus was the capital of Syria (Isa. 7:8) situated northeast of the Sea of Galilee and east of the Mediterranean on the edge of the anti-Lebanon mountain range. It grew along the northeastern slope of Mt. Hermon and still dwells in its shadow. The city was an important trade center in antiquity because of the highway that joined three major caravan routes. These routes made trade possible between Egypt, Arabia and Mesopotamia. One route took the goods of the city to the Mediterranean (about 100 km. to the west) via the city of Tyre in Lebanon. The eastern route led along the Fertile Crescent to Babylonian and Assyrian territory (now the Persian Gulf states). The southern route led to Egypt via ancient Israel.

The area of the city was famous for several local products. It was known for the export of "damask" a patterned cloth. The area was rich agriculturally with water sources from the Abana and the Pharpar rivers. Its rich source of water was far superior to the river Jordan of Israel which caused Naaman the leper (captain of the host of Syria) to despise the instruction of Elisha to dip himself in the Jordan for his healing (II Kings 5:12).

Damascus was occupied by Neolithic times (probably because of the water supply). By the time of Abraham (2000 BCE) the city was well established. The Bible records that Abraham defeated a coalition of kings nearby (Gen. 14:15). Later, King David conquered Syria and Damascus was garrisoned during his rule. Under Solomon Damascus was lost to Rezon of Zobah (for a more complete view of the story read 2 Sam. 8; 1 Chron. 18; 1 Kings 11). The state of Aram was formed with Damascus as its capital city. The dynasty of Rezin (Hezion and Tabrimmon) increased the strength of the Aramean Kingdom.

The conflicts of Aramean Damascus give it frequent Biblical mention. By the time of the fourth generation of Rezin's dynasty, the king of Israel (the Northern Tribe confederation) King Ahab entered into an agreement with Ben-Hadad II. The Bible records the agreement was against God's will and Ahab was later on killed in battle against Syria (1 Kings 20:32,34,42; 22:35,37). Ben-Hadad raised the largest army (20,000 soldiers) contingent at the indecisive battle of Qarqar (against Assyrian domination).

The prophet Elijah was sent by the LORD to anoint Hazael as the next king of Damascus (1 Kings 19:15). The prophet Elisha later on prophesied to king Hazael that he would be king of Damascus and that he would do great harm to the children of Israel (2 Kings 8:12). The prophets Isaiah, Jeremiah and Amos record prophecies of the destruction of Damascus and Syria (which occurred in 732 BCE) by King Tiglath-Pileser of Assyria (Isaiah 8:4; Jeremiah 49:23-27; Amos 1:4).

In addition to the connection to the Northern tribes, Damascus had an impact on Judah as well. When King Ahaz (grandson of Uzziah) was king of Judah, he made an evil pact with King Tiglath-pileser III (king of Assyria) to protect him against Syria and Israel. Ahaz went to pay homage to Tiglath-pileser who had overthrown Damascus and while there saw an altar which he later duplicated and placed in the temple in Jerusalem (2 Kings 16:10, 14,16).

After the Assyrian destruction of the city (used as an illustration by Isaiah to Judah, cp. Isa. 8:4) it became a vassal greatly reduced in population and importance. Though still of economic importance in the region, it became a part of the satrapy of Hamath (Ezek. 27:18). With the coming of Alexander the Great to the region, the city gained more importance. During the Seleucis period it was a trade location, but much less important than Antioch, nearer to the Mediterranean. Restored briefly as capital of the province in 111 BCE under Antiochus IX Roman period, Damascus was eventually taken by Aretas the Nabatean until lost to Tigranes the Armenian in 85 BCE. It fell victim to Roman expansion by 64 BCE and was a well-known city of the Decapolis during the life of Jesus.

By the time of Paul's visit, Aretas IV (9 BCE- 40 CE) was ethnarch of the city. Damascus is first mentioned in Acts as the destination that Paul was going to when he had his conversion. He was on his way to the city with letters of permission from the officials in Jerusalem permitting him to imprison and persecute the new believers of 'The Way' (Acts 9:1-8). Paul arrived in Damascus a believer in Jesus but blind from the experience and lived in the house of Judas. God sent a believer named Ananias to restore his sight (Acts 9:10-22). Thereafter, Paul began to preach in Damascus and ended up fleeing the city because the Jews there desired to kill him (Acts 9:25; 2 Corinthians 11:32-33). Later, in his letter to the Galatians, Paul testified of having gone to Damascus for a period of time, after which he went to Jerusalem to see the Apostles (Galatians 1:17).

Derbe

Acts 14:20-21

Southeast of Lystra some thirty miles distance was the small town of Derbe. In the Lycaonian District, this town was at the extreme edge of cities considered "Galatian". The town was small, but the work of Paul and Barnabas yielded a number of followers. Among them, Gaius was converted and much later joined Paul's team on the Third Mission Journey (cp. Acts 20:4).

Following the strengthening that no doubt resulted from the encouragement of the growth in the movement at Derbe, Paul and Barnabas journeyed back to Lystra and Iconium (45 miles northwest), in spite of their prior reception (Acts 14:21-22) and strengthened the small flock of believers in each place. Paul and Silas made their way to Derbe on the Second Journey (Acts 16:1).

Attempts to locate the exact site of the ancient village have been attempted by M. Balance in 1956 and 1964. His identification favors a small outcropping four kilometers south east of Kerti Huyuk.

Ephesus

(Acts 18:19-19:1; 20:31; Ephesians; 1 Tim. 1:3; 2 Tim. 1:16-18; 4:14-19; 1 Cor. 15:32; Rev. 1:11; 2:1-7)

Historians use terms to describe the ancient city of Ephesus like "the supreme metropolis of Asia" which reflects evidence of a highly developed city. By the time of the New Testament it was a city that had become a cultural and religious memory, a yesterday romance, not unlike Paris in the modern world. Filled with the symbols of greatness, but struggling in the economics of a changing world and a troublesome silting harbor, the bustling city continued to play a significant role, but was fading with time.

Location: Ephesus was constructed on a river bend that was eventually dredged into a full harbor near the mouth of the Cayster River, on the western coast of Asia Minor (modern Turkey). Along the coastal plain between Smyrna to the north and Miletus to the south, the site is now about six miles from the Aegean Sea. The city shifted in five distinct locations over time, each within a small area. The Apostles Paul and John were familiar with the city that scholars have dubbed "Ephesus III" the largest (in area) of the five. The areas where Ephesus located are as follows: Ephesus I: Aya Suluk (St. John Area); Ephesus II: Artemission area; Ephesus III: Port of St. Paul: base of Mount

Koressos; Ephesus IV: north of Aya Suluk; Ephesus V: Selçuk area.

Because of the man-made harbor structure and the flow of the river, a backwash flow caused the harbor to frequently silt up (by 449 BCE we already read of problems documented about the silting. Later, Eusebius records that Ephesus honored Emperor Hadrian for dredging and making navigable the harbor). When cleared, Ephesus was in a location that justified a great seaport. The city sat at the convergence of three land routes with a shipping lane from the north via the channel created by the Island of Chios and an opening facing the cities of Macedonia. The land routes that converged on Ephesus included: 1) The Colossae / Laodicea road (travelling east), 2) The road to Sardis and Galatia (northeast), and 3) The Smyrna (north) main road.

Population: Some scholars estimate the number of people living at Ephesus to have exceeded 250,000 inhabitants during Ephesus III, which would make it perhaps the fourth largest of its day behind: 1) Rome; 2) Alexandria; and 3) Antioch. This large a city was an economic stronghold in Asia Minor, and justified the title "supreme metropolis of Asia" though there is evidence that its overall economic standing may have been slowly declining.

Archaic Period (900-560 BCE): The foundations of the city may date back to the waves of Sea Peoples and resistance movements that characterized part of the Archaic Period. A village developed though it was not as well developed or known as Miletus. It appears to have played a significant role as part of the Ionian Renaissance during the time of Heraclitus the philosopher. It was a farming and trade village until the harbor was established. A significant cultic site to Cybele developed there.

Note on Cybele: Originally an Astarte-like warrior-goddess associated with the sacred axe labrys, but later assimilated with the Anatolian Earth Mother Goddess. Little is known of the cultic worship until much later, when the cult was brought to Rome in 205 BCE. The later version required the accession of self-emasculated priests known as "galli". Another aspect of the cultic

*worship was the use of immersion in the blood of a bull,
a practice later taken over by Mithraism.*

Greco-Lydian Period (560-290 BCE): According to Herodotus
(I.26), King Croessus (560 BCE) conquered the city mid 6th
century BCE, as he tamed the Ionian cities. The establishment
of mining operations for gold and the minting of Lydian coins in
this period gave rise to trade that can be archaeologically
documented. During this period the city re-engineered the
Cybele cultic site and built a Temple to the Greek goddess
Artemis, constructed entirely of marble.

In 546 BCE, the area became part of the Satrapy of Ionia. When
Darius died (485), the Persian King's son Xerxes focused his
conquest ambition on Greek territory. On a return from battles in
Greece he honored the Temple of Artemis in 478 BCE, an
unusual move as the Persians destroyed many other
contemporary shrines. The Persians were eventually defeated in
the region in 466 BCE, when Ephesus became a tributary of
Athens. The city undertook to restore the Artemission, and the
city in 450 BCE.

As the center for tourism and trade, the Artemission became
synonymous with Ephesus. After the tragic fire in 356 BCE
(tradition holds that Herostratos set that temple aflame to make
a name for himself), the city took a long time to recover.
Alexander would later offer to finish the half-reconstructed
Temple, but the city declined, not completing the work until
Lysimachus held the city upon Alexander's death. Lysimachus
introduced new colonists and renamed city after his wife
Arsinoë, but name didn't last. He increased the prominence of
the city by enclosing it with six miles of wall. (Today, the
traditional "Prison of Paul" is located within westernmost tower of
that wall).

Greco-Roman Period (290 BCE-300 CE): After Lysimachus was
killed in 281 BCE; Ephesus came under control of Seleucid
dynasty. They were defeated by the Romans at Magnesia (189
BCE) and Ephesus was turned over to control by Pergamum,
until in 133 BCE Ephesus came under direct Roman rule.

The site was a known Roman haven, as a discovery of a statue of Julius Caesar suggests, along with a record that Antony and Cleopatra wintered there (33/32 BCE). The erection of an Egyptian style Serapis temple at the northeast corner of the Agora may have been by Cleopatra. A famous colossal head identified as Antony has also been found. The Austrian excavation team found a stone head now universally accepted as that of the Egyptian god Amon. Not always a period of comfortable relations, Ephesus didn't like Rome initially when Roman civil wars helped Brutus and Cassius then Antony. Hailed by Pliny as "the great luminary of Asia" and by Strabo as "the greatest emporium of Asia", the city enjoyed frequent foreign guests, and built its tourism industry.

Later emperors also enjoyed a relationship with the city. Statuary dedicated to Augustus in the temple of Artemis is depicted on coinage. The monumental triple gate to the commercial agora from the Library of Celsus was dedicated to Augustus' family in 4/3 BCE. Augustus also regulated the scope and size of the legal "area of refuge for criminals at the Artemission" in hopes of stopping the city from becoming overloaded with criminals. Later, Nero rebuilt the stadium and Ephesus coined a commemorative coin in honor of his work. Nero was not embarrassed to openly take statuary from the city for his own collection.

Emperor Domitian (81-96 CE), who exiled John to Patmos, is credited by some as having erected a great altar and temple to himself on Curetes Street. When Domitian was assassinated in 96, the colossal statue was destroyed, pieces are found in the Museum at Izmir. Trajan also took a special interest in the city. His father had been appointed the proconsul of Asia back in 79 and built a wall around the Artemission precinct. Trajan added to his father's old work a new showpiece: the Nymphaion on Curetes street.

After the time of Paul and John, Emperor Hadrian made Ephesus his "favorite city" and entitled it the "Imperial Capital of Asia" (125 CE). He instituted games called "Hadrianea" and local sponsors held the games in his honor. A Neocorate temple was built and dedicated to Hadrian in 129 CE. The citizens of Ephesus honored Emperor Antonius Pius on his birthday and he built a great gymnasium in response. The city was eventually destroyed by the Goth invasion of 262 CE, and it never regained any real importance.

Galatia (Region)

Acts 16:6; 18:23; 1 Corinthians 16:1; Galatians 1:2; 2 Timothy 4:10; 1 Peter 1:1

Galatia originally received its name from Celtic tribes of Gaul who settled in its later northern region around 275 BCE. It seems the increase in European population and their attacks in Greece and Macedonia brought the *Keltoi* or *Keltai* southward; and their assistance to the Bithynian king, Nikomedes I in a civil war brought them east to where they eventually settled. In 25 BCE their last dynastic king (Amyntas) died and both the northern and added southern region were made into the Roman province of Galatia.

Located in central Asia Minor the modern capital city of Ankara, Turkey is within the region's once held territory. Though having no coastline it was a prosperous and powerful kingdom in its day. During the reign of its kings it contained at times sections of Pontus, Pisidia, Lycaonia, Phrygia, Isauria and Paphlagonia, as well as the area earlier settled by the Gauls.

The Apostle Paul visited this region during all three of his missionary journeys, though only traveling to the southern cities of Derbe, Lystra, Iconium, and Pisidian Antioch. The exact destination of Paul's writings to the church in Galatia is uncertain, whether to the broader historic Gallic region or the newly established Roman province (much more limited in size but contemporary to Paul). No visit to the northern region by Paul is recorded in the Book of Acts.

Greece

Zechariah 9:13 Acts 20:2; Grecia: Daniel 8:21; 10:20; 11:2; Grecians (Greeks): Joel 3:6; Grecians (Greek-speaking Jews): Acts 6:1; 9:29. Greeks: Acts 14:1; 17:4, 12; 18:4,17; 19:10,17; 20:21; 21:28. Greek: Acts 16:1,3; 21:37.

The Greeks (or Hellenes) are normally defined as a blended people from a series of tribal incursions that occurred into the Balkan Peninsula which begun in the 12th Century BCE. Tribes of Pelasgeans (that settled the Boetia and Ellas areas of modern central Greece) and the Achaens (that settled in the plains of Thessaly and river basins of Macedonia – modern northern Greece) were pushed by early movement waves of other tribes. People known today as the Ionians (early Indo-Europeans), and later Dorians (Indo-Europeans that entered the area from Germany and Austria from about 1100 BCE) moved southward from European lands and settled on both sides of the Aegean Sea.

The settlements are traced in four specific movements. The Bronze Age (3000-1100 BCE) are represented by four different areas where excavations have unearthed the Greek beginnings: The Cycladic Island Civilizations of Achaens; The Minoan subculture, named after the legendary King Minos of Crete; the Mycenaean subculture named after the ancient Peloponnesian city; and the city of Troy uncovered in Heinrich Schliemann's excavations (now northwestern Turkey). The traditional date of the "Trojan War" was 1194 BCE, and memories of the contemporary cities are recalled in the later composed Homeric Epics, The Iliad and The Odyssey. These four early subcultures are all part of ancient formation of the people we call the "Greeks" today.

As the Greeks settled throughout the Mediterranean and Black Sea coastal areas (750-550 BCE), the ruling of these cities changed from a monarchy to a more democratic form of government. Their society began to show a greater development in the arts, language and philosophy, but they failed to ally their city-states and settlements into a strong political unit, which made them prone to enemy attacks. The Persians came in the 5th century, and took by force many Greek city-states along the eastern Aegean coast, but Greek city-states (polis) eventually fought them off at Marathon (490 BCE) and Salamis (480 BCE).

Philip II of Macedon was a regent of a child king, and had him killed, assuming the throne of the Macedonians. Devising significant improvements in contemporary warfare and weaponry, he overtook the Greeks and unified them, destroying the "polis" or city state style rulership after more than a thousand years of its domination. Philip planned to march across the Hellespont (the waterway that separates Europe and Asia) but was assassinated, leaving the throne to his son Alexander (later called "the Great"). Alexander spread Greek culture throughout the Persian Empire, Egypt, the Levant, Asia Minor, and Mesopotamia. He successfully conquered the entire Kingdom of the Medes and Persians, as well as parts of India and territories that today are part of the Arabia Gulf states. Even Kandahar in Afghanistan is a corruption of his name.

With the conquest of Alexander came the spread of a common thought and language throughout these areas. When Alexander died (323 BCE), the lands were divided between four of his generals (called the "Diadoche" or successors). Naturally "Hellenizing" the lands they ruled they formed a more unified infrastructure of the territories. The universalizing of the koinē Greek language ("Common Dialect", a simplified version of Attic Greek) allowed the Gospel to be transported to many people in many places. Commentators of the New Testament note that this allowed the message of the Gospel to rapidly spread in these territories.

It was not only a common language and new form of government that the Greeks developed, but also the speculative mind. Their history of rhetoric and philosophy, were hallmarks of Greek culture and introduced the world to a different type of thinking. Beginning with Ionian Philosophers like Thales of Miletus (6th Century BCE), many Greeks had moved from "superstitious" based answers for cause and effect to observation sciences. The spreading of the Greek culture not only brought unification to many peoples, but also raised a standard of material culture throughout the eastern Mediterranean as seen through many archaeological finds and ruins.

It seems Paul even used the term "Greek" to be a synonym for "civilized non-Jews" in Romans 10:12 and Galatians 3:28. This allowed Paul to distinguish between the Jews (circumcised) and the non-Jews, called Gentiles (uncircumcised), but also left a category for the "barbarians" that often warred with the Romans in the northern areas of the Empire. The word "Greeks" in the New Testament can be used in various ways, including referring to people of the Hellenic race or at times simply civilized Gentiles. Many of the Greeks in the Book of Acts were in fact proselytes to Judaism, who were subsequently led to Jesus by Paul. Hence the word "Grecians" in the New Testament is often a reference to Greek-speaking Jews many of whom were scattered by the Dispersion or Gentiles that were proselytes.

The term "Greece" is only mentioned once in Acts 20:2, and appears to be referring to Achaia, the Roman province that embraces the southern part of today's modern Greece. The Romans used the term "Achaia" to speak sometimes of Greece on the whole, and other times with specific reference to the southern portion that was beforehand a region of Greece. Achaia is mentioned several times in the New Testament (Acts 18:12, 27; Romans 15:26; 16:5; 1 Thess. 1:7,8); Paul visited it and Macedonia (Acts19: 21).

Athens was known for its philosophy and learning in ancient times. Paul encountered this culture at Mars' Hill in his speech to the Areopagites (17:16-18:1). Though the results of Paul's ministry in the city were meager (a few came to Jesus) the church at Athens did flourish. He also traveled and spent eighteen months in Corinth (18:1), the province's capital. He left the Second Mission Journey via the Greek port of Cenchrea (18:18) and again visited Greece during his Third Missionary Journey as well (20:2-3).

Hierapolis

Col. 1:5-8; 4:12-13; Philemon 23

A few miles north of Laodicea in the Lycus Valley, the ruins of Hierapolis stand along the ancient roadway connecting Laodicea to Philadelphia and Sardis to the northwest. The ruins demonstrate it was a prosperous trade center built around hot springs that were considered a source of healing power in the Roman period. In the southwestern edge of the Phrygian territory, the city is perched 250 feet above on a natural terrace overlooking the surrounding valley. The ancient city had all the drawing points of a resort, with all the regional goods of the other regional cities: wools, dying trades and textiles.

With hot thermal springs ever present and cool mountain air to offer cold water constantly available, the dying guilds no doubt made use of these natural features required in adding color to cloth. The city also had an advantage in the bath complex, still seen on the northwestern part of the city's edge, near the northern necropolis. Some scholars compare the hot water of Hierapolis, and the cold water of Colossae to the lukewarm water of Laodicea as the background for the imagery of Rev. 3:15-16.

Hierapolis was not a great city of antiquity, but was likely a pagan cult center as demonstrated in the name, which means "holy city". A Hellenistic theatre demonstrates the city existed well before the earthquake of 17 CE, when Augustus supplied some aid to restoring the city. Inscriptions show there was a significant Jewish presence in the city. Another damaging quake came in 60 CE, affecting the Lycus cities, and requiring aid from Emperor Nero. The city may have been reached by Paul's ministry impact from Ephesus (Acts 19:10), but more likely came under the evangelistic preaching of Epaphras (cp. Col. 4:12-13; see Laodicea and Colossae).

Stoic philosopher Epictetus stayed in the city for some time, as did Papias. Polycrates, Bishop of Ephesus (190 CE) is quoted by Eusebius (Church History 3.31) as stating that the Apostle Philip was buried in the city, though scholars debate whether the reference is to the Apostle or the evangelist.

The site today includes two partially restored ancient baths (north and south of the city), an impressive colonnaded street, a Temple of Apollo and the Martyrium of St. Philip. The nearby hot springs at Pamukkale, or "cotton castle" (named because of the white calcified hot springs) are not to be missed!

Iconium

Acts 14:1-7

In the central plateau of the Lycaonian District, Iconium was a city set amidst a very large fertile plain that stretched to the north and east. Well watered and surrounded by an unusually productive and stoneless alluvial soil, the farms of the region are still some of modern Turkey's finest for grains, orchards of plums and apricots. Ramsey noted that the historian Strabo was struck by the difference between the barren fields of the Lycaonian plains, and the lush area around Iconium. He concluded that the intelligent use of irrigation probably made the difference, since they were both subject to similar weather patterns.

The actual founding of the city is uncertain, but it is clear that the city was proud of its Greek heritage. By 25 BCE, Iconium was brought under the Roman province of Galatia. Holding on to their Greek heritage, Dr. Luke assigns the name "Hellenes" to this people in his writing.

The city was connected by a roadway to Pisidian Antioch some eighty miles to the northwest and had good lines of trade and communication. It was a Greek minded community with a significant but not dominant Jewish community. As a more democratic and Greek metropolis, resistance against Paul and Barnabas was not swift and decisive as in places with dominant leadership structures. In this city some of this community stirred up mobs against Paul's message, but Paul was evidently able to manage the unrest for a period. The team remained in place, and saw considerable success in their preaching. After a spell of success, another mob began to stir. Unlike Pisidian Antioch, where the aristocrats expelled Paul and his companion, the mob of the Hellenes was stirred and eventually threatened to stone them. Barnabas and Paul fled the city south to Lystra and Derbe.

In addition to Paul's first visit to Iconium, he returned on the Second Journey and possibly on the third (Acts 16:1-4; 18:23). Certain of the Jewish community followed Paul from Iconium and harassed him again in Lystra, pushing the crowd to stone him (Acts 14:19). Paul recalls the problems he had in Galatia in his late writings (2 Tim. 3:11). Paul's concerns over the perversion to the Gospel message were directed at this and the surrounding communities in the Epistle to the Galatians. In addition, Peter's first Epistle was likely written to this city, along with Lystra, Derbe and Antioch of Pisidia (1 Pet. 1:1).

Jerusalem

Acts 1:4,8,12,19; 2:5,14; 4:6,16; 5:16,28; 6:7; 8:1,14,25,26,27; 9:2,13,21,26,28; 10: 39; 11:2,22,27; 12:25; 13:13,27,31; 15:2,4; 16:4; 18:21; 19:21; 20:16,22:21:4,11,12,13,15,17,31; 22:5,17,18; 23:11,24:11; 25:1,3,7,9,15,20,24; 26:4,10,20; 28:17; Joshua 10:1,3,5; 12:10; 15:8; Judges 1:7,8,21; 19:10; II Samuel 5:6; I Kings 2:41; 3:1; II Kings 8:17,26;Ezra 1:2,3; Psalms 51:18; 68:29; 102:21; 137:5,6,7; Isaiah 1:1; Jeremiah 52:21; Matthew 21:1,10; 23:37; Mark 1:5; 3:8,22; Luke 2:22,25,38,41,42,43,45; 4:9; 21:20; John 1:19; 2:13; 4:20; 10:22; Romans 15:19,25,26,31;ICorinthians 16:3;Galatians 1:17,18;2:1;4:25,26; Hebrews 12:22; Revelations 3:12; 21:2,10

"Jerusalem" is a compound word that is literally translated "city of peace". It is the holy city of the Bible, the capital of the United Kingdom of Israel under from the time King David moved from Hebron. After the division of the Kingdom, Jerusalem was maintained as the capital of the southern tribal confederation of Judah. Most often the city appears in reference to the historical events of the Bible, but at times the prophets used its name in reference to the idealized future city of Messiah's throne.

Jerusalem probably first appears in the Bible as the "Salem" of Melchisedek the priest-king in Genesis 14:18. Later the Bible directly speaks of Jerusalem during the Israelite conquest of Canaan under the leadership of Joshua (Joshua 10:14). The Israelites were unable to take the fortified city even though the surrounding cities were captured. This area was allotted to the tribe of Judah as an inheritance, but not brought under control of the Israelites until the time of David. During the conquest the city was the stronghold of Jebus (named for the Jebusites that inhabited the city). The initial city of Jebus that was conquered is now entirely located outside the walls of today's "Old City", and is beneath the southern extremity of the Ophel ridge in the village of Silwan.

With the rise of King David, Israel's ruler captured Jebus and moved the throne to this more centrally located city (after seven years in Hebron). After Saul ruled from "Gibeah of Saul", David found that by taking a city from the Jebusites it could literally become known as the "city of David". More significant than just a capital city was the establishment of a spiritual center for the people of Israel. With the rise of the Temple under Solomon the city became the spiritual or religious center of the children of Israel.

Jerusalem was less than an ideal setting for trade. It was never situated directly on a caravan route or major trade route and had no seaport to aid in trade. Though commerce was more difficult, it was a city with significant natural defenses. Jerusalem was constructed on a series of mountain ridges. Large valleys surround the ancient city: to the east was the Kidron Valley, to the west and south was the Hinnom. Ravines hindered attack (Ps. 125:2) in every direction but from the north, where the city was historically most vulnerable. To the north of Jebus was a threshing floor, later chosen to place the ancient Temple (2 Chronicles 3:1). The site of the former Temple is now occupied by the Moslem structure called the "Dome of the Rock" built in 691 CE.

Jerusalem reached its pinnacle of glory during King Solomon's rule. It was Solomon who built the Temple of the Lord and then built himself a royal. The Bible records that Jerusalem and King Solomon enjoyed world fame during this time, as Solomon's wisdom was sought out and many nations brought lavish and expensive gifts in honor of the God of Israel who had given its king such wisdom. This glorious time was short lived.

Israel was cut in two by his sons after the death of Solomon. Jerusalem remained the capital city of the two southern tribes, Judah and Benjamin. Initially the city of Shechem and later the city of Samaria became the capital city of the Northern Kingdom of Israel. Despite this split, many from the northern tribes still traveled to Jerusalem to worship. As a result, the Kings of the northern tribes sought to build up high places within their territory.

Jerusalem was attacked during the onslaught of the Assyrians (722 BCE) that led to the fall of the Northern Kingdom, but was not destroyed. Eventually the city fell under King Nebuchadnezzar of Babylon in 586 BCE. During the siege, the Temple was burned and the walls of the city pulled down. The articles of the Temple were taken to Babylon and the people taken as exiles to Babylon.

In their Persian exile the passion for Jerusalem became evident among the Jewish people according to the writings of the period. Psalms 137 relates a longing for Jerusalem:

"By the rivers of Babylon, there we sat down, yea, we wept, when we remembered Zion.... How shall we sing the LORD's song in a strange land: If I forget thee, O Jerusalem, let my right hand forget *her cunning*. If I do not remember thee, let my tongue cleave to the roof of my mouth; if I prefer not Jerusalem above my chief joy."(Ps. 137 selected).

After two generations in captivity, Cyrus of Persia conquered Babylon and made a declaration (circa 538 BCE) that allowed the people of Israel to return to Jerusalem and rebuild their temple (Ezra 1:2-4). The Temple was rebuilt in twenty years under the leadership of Zerubbabel. Later, another group of Jews returned to Jerusalem and rebuilt the wall of Jerusalem under the leadership of Nehemiah. It was built with much opposition but was completed in just fifty-two days (Nehemiah 6:15). The city was revived under the Persians, and began to take shape again as a vassal city.

In the fourth century, Alexander the Great conquered the Persian Empire and (as a result) took over Jerusalem. With him came the Greek culture and way of thinking which was completely contrary to the Jewish way and worship. Greeks celebrated multiple gods and had great respect for pictures and statues to represent deities. The Jewish people were "aniconic" and were repulsed by the notion of polytheism. Under Alexander and the Greek domination, the city shuddered in discomfort, but continued to grow. After his death the region was held by the Ptolemy family for a time, and grew in stature and importance. It was after the defeat of the Ptolemies by the Seleucid Dynasty (ruling from Syria) that the troubles opened into revolt. A

Seleucid named Antiochus IV was particularly zealous in spreading Greek culture and defiled the Temple at Jerusalem, leading to a revolt in the streets of the city.

This revolt led to full-scale rebellion, which culminated in a series of battles led by the five sons of a Judean priest named Matthais. The sons became known as the Maccabees, after the nickname of the oldest son Judas "Maccabeus" (the hammer). The Maccabees succeeded in recapturing Jerusalem and the Temple and had it cleansed of the Greek desecration. The temple was rededicated, a time recalled in the "Feast of Dedication" or "Hanukkah" (cp. John 10:22).

After the Maccabees, Jerusalem was for a time a capital under the hands of the Jews for a short time, but eventually fell (as did every other kingdom of the time) to the rise of Rome. The Romans ruled the city by appointing Jewish leaders as kings when possible (like Herod the Great and his descendants) and later took the city under direct Roman rule of Procurators (like Pontius Pilate).

During the Roman Period, the Temple in Jerusalem was expanded by Herod the Great and was in use during the time of Jesus and His apostles (but still under construction). The city was a pilgrimage center, where the Jews would travel to worship and celebrate the various Jewish feasts. Jesus traveled to Jerusalem throughout His life (i.e. at the age of twelve He astonished the leaders in the temple with the wisdom and knowledge that he had - Luke 2:47). Later in His ministry, He "cleansed the Temple" by throwing out the money (John 2:14-16). The Gospels record a number of travels to Jerusalem for the various Feasts (John 7:14-39). One particularly moving scene included reference to Jesus who cried over Jerusalem as "a city that kills the prophets and those sent to her" (Matthew 24:23-25:13). He told his disciples that He would be killed in Jerusalem (Matthew 16:21; Luke 9:31) and predicted the fall of Jerusalem in 70 AD (Luke 21: 5-24). He warned His Disciples not to leave Jerusalem before the gift of the Holy Spirit had been poured out on them (Luke 24:49). Jesus instructed them to begin from Jerusalem (Luke 24:47).

The Temple was completed just before 67 CE, and was destroyed three years later when Titus sacked the city to quell a revolt. Jews were taken captive to Rome and other Roman cities as slaves, martyrs, and sport for the Roman arenas where they were killed by men and eaten by lions as sport.

Jerusalem is the setting for the opening stories in the Book of Acts. The story began with the Ascension on the Mount of Olives, where Luke records the commission of Jesus to the Disciples "to be witnesses unto me both in Jerusalem, and in all Judea, and in Samaria, and unto the uttermost part of the earth." Luke's first portion included all Jerusalem stories, including the choosing of Matthais (Acts 1), the coming of the Holy Spirit at Pentecost (or Shavuot - Acts 2), the rise of the Messianic leadership (Acts 3 and 4) and the early conflicts of the Messianic rise (Acts 5-6).

One of the external conflicts that arose in Jerusalem was the persecution of believers by the Temple leadership. These conflicts included the arrest of Peter and John, who were set free in miraculous ways (Acts 5:19; 12:7-11) after being imprisoned. The persecution of believers climaxed with the stoning to death of the Deacon Stephen (Acts 7-8:3) and the martyrdom of James (the brother of John) by the hand of Herod Agrippa I (Acts 12:2). This resulted in the dispersion of the believers abroad, who went everywhere preaching the Gospel. Paul (much later) was also among those who underwent persecution in Jerusalem, which led him to be taken to Rome for trial, where he later on died. Even with the persecution and the scattering of the believers, some of the Apostles were left in Jerusalem and the city became the center for the Church Council, which comprised of Apostles and the elders (Acts15: 2,6,19-29).

Until the removal of the Messianic believers from access to the Temple funds paid to the poor and widows, the Temple was the major relief agency for Jews. Offerings paid at the Temple helped Jews in Jerusalem and in the Diaspora. After the Temple leadership suspended the access to these funds, the believers established their own funds in the hands of Deacons (Acts 6). As a result, Paul often received offerings even from the Gentile churches to take to the poor congregation in Jerusalem (Acts 24:17). On one occasion relief came to the Deacons in Jerusalem from the church at Antioch, which received a prophecy that there would be famine throughout the earth (Acts 11:28,29,30). The offering was not to be used just in Jerusalem, but to believers everywhere. The new system took the place of the Temple relief in the lives of the poor, the widows and orphans of the growing believing community in Jerusalem and in the other communities abroad.

Jerusalem was sometimes prophetically idealized in Scripture (Psalm 48:1,2; 50:1-6; Jeremiah 33:14,15,16; Zechariah 8:1-8). The city was the setting from which the Messiah's promised reign will commence in John's vision of the millennial rule (Revelations 20:9). The Apocalypse depicts Jerusalem as an eternal city (Revelations 21:22).

Joppa

Joshua 19:46; 2 Chronicles 2, 16; Ezra 3:7; Jonah 1:3; Acts 8, 9, 10, 11

Joppa (also Jaffa, Yafo) was an ancient port city of the eastern Mediterranean. The city may have gained its name as the traditional burial place of Japheth (Yefet) son of Noah, or perhaps a reference to its beauty (Hebrew: yafa). The archaeological mound of Jaffa is today a suburb of Tel Aviv (a modern city) and still has a significant population (which makes access to the ancient ruins impossible). In antiquity, this was Jerusalem's seaport (35 miles away) and was the only significant ancient port in the area prior to Caesarea (a later rival seaport built by Herod the Great). It was the only natural harbor on the Mediterranean between Mt. Carmel and Egypt, and the city was built on a rocky cape overlooking the sea (which rose about 120 feet above sea level). The cliff made a reasonably secure defense and the location of the port offered a commercial trading base. Though there were reefs about less than 400 feet from the shore, boats could still enter from the north. Sandy beaches nearby allowed the shallow crafts to come ashore. Additionally, the city was supplied by two water springs.

Joppa was an administrative city of the Egyptian rule in Canaan until it was taken over by the tribe of Dan as an inheritance (Joshua 19:46). The Philistines held Joppa for a time and made it their northern seaport, but it became part of the kingdom of

Israelite Kings David and Solomon. Under Solomon it became the transit port to bring all the cedar needed for the construction of the Temple at Jerusalem and the king's palace (2 Chronicles 2:16). After Solomon (and the division of the kingdom), it appears to have largely reverted to Philistine control.

Uzziah of Judah (769-733 BCE) took the city just prior to the call of the prophet Jonah, who ran from the command of the Lord to go and preach to Nineveh and boarded a ship at this port according to the Biblical record. King Hezekiah revolted from the grip of the Assyrians after the death of Sargon II (705 BCE) and allied with King Sidqia of Ashkelon, who occupied Joppa. During the raid to quench rebellion in the rule of Sennacherib the port was laid waste. Sennacharib's prism mentioned the city: "I besieged Beth-Dagan, Jaffa, Bene Beraq, Asor and the cities of Sidqia, I conquered and spoiled them."

The city was rebuilt and again used as a seaport to bring in logs for the rebuilding of the Temple at Jerusalem during the time of Ezra (Ezra 3:7). With the rise of the Greeks the city passed from the hands of Alexander, who proclaimed it a colony to the General Ptolemy I (301 BCE) of Egypt. The Ptolemy dynasty held the port until 197 BCE when they were defeated by the Seleucid kingdom. Antiochus IV the Seleucid used Joppa as his military base to fight against Judea in his bid to Hellenize the region. Judas Macabeus (a priestly ruler and warrior of Judea) unsuccessfully tried to capture the port. Jonathan (his youngest brother and successor) captured the port for short time. Simon (another Maccabean ruler) was able to capture Joppa and turn it into an all-Jewish city (2 Mac. 12).

As the Roman Empire swallowed Judea, Pompeii declared Joppa a free port (63BC). It was returned to the Jews in 47 BCE by Julius Caesar, and offered to Herod the Great ten years later.

In the book of Acts, Joppa was home to a number of believers including Dorcas, who Peter raised from the dead (Acts 9:36-42). It was also in Joppa that Peter, on the house of Simon the tanner, received the vision of the unclean foods in the sheet – a vision that signaled the opening of the gospel to both Jew and Gentile. It was from Joppa that he was commanded to go Cornelius the centurion (Acts10: 9-16) who waited to hear the message in Caesarea. A generation after Peter's visit, Joppa was involved in the Jewish revolts against Rome and was destroyed by Cestuis Gallus (67-8 CE). Two small homes that suffered this destruction can still be seen in the central square excavation in the port area.

Laodicea

Col. 1:7, 4:12-13, 16; Rev. 1:11, 3:14-22

The last of the seven churches of Revelation was that of Laodicea. As a crossroad of two important roads, this city had an important commercial and logistical position. The road that carried John's letter began at Ephesus, and moved north through Smyrna and Pergamum before turning east to Thyatira. Dropping due south, the letters were carried to Sardis, then southeast to Philadelphia and finally Laodicea. Evidence of the ancient road demonstrates that it continued to Colossae and eventually to the Mediterranean port at Attalia (Antalya).

Intersecting with the Pergamum – Attalia road was an inland roadway from Cappadocia via Apamea (due east of Laodicea). This road gently eased down to the coast at Ephesus, some 160 kilometers away. Ten miles east of the city lay the remains of Colossae, an important city in the writing and ministry of the Apostle Paul.

Established in the C3 BCE by the Seleucid Antiochus II, the city was named after his wife Laodice. Built on the Lycus Tributary of the Meander River, it was surnamed "Laodicea on Lycus", to distinguish it from other similarly named cities. The city was apparently addressed with the nearby cities of Hierapolis and Colossae (Col. 2:1; 4:13-16) and was no doubt linked in trade and commerce with those cities.

Though reasonably strong from the trade in what Strabo referred to as "raven-black wool" and its thriving agricultural base, the city did need the assistance of Rome after an earthquake disabled the city in 60 CE, according to Tacitus. The garment industry recovered, and competed with Hierapolis and Colossae for the textile manufacture and sale. There was also development of a medical industry, based on the eye salves and

"Phrygian powders" used in eye treatment (cp. Rev. 3:15-16). The banking and money exchange industry also thrived in the city, an ironic reality of the city that was called "poor and naked and blind!"

Positioned in the Lycus Valley a few miles from the hot calcium waters of modern Pammukale, the tell affords a view to the north and east of the hot waters that pour out of the earth, and the distant snow capped mountains to the south. Drawing the hot water from a distance of more than four miles away, the water would arrive to the city lukewarm, and need to be reheated. Many have noted the irony of Rev. 3:15.

The church of Laodicea was begun by Epaphras while Paul was at Ephesus (cp. Acts 19:10). The New Testament offers no direct evidence of a visit by Paul to the city, though he refers to believers there in the letter to Colossae. The "letter to Laodicea" did not survive (Col. 4:16).

Lasea

Acts 27:8

Lasea was a town apparently in close proximity to the harbor at Fair Havens (according to Acts 27:8). The site has been identified with a ruin about eight kilometers inland. Some scholars believe it was the same town as "Lasos", mentioned by Pliny in Natural History (4.59), but this is not universally accepted. Little excavation has been completed in the Matala cape region (the central southern coast) of Crete thus far.

Lycaonia

Lycaonia: Acts 14:6, 11. Lystra: Acts 14:6, 8, 21; 16:1, 2; 2 Tim. 3:11. Derbe: Acts 14:6, 20; 16:1; 20:4.

Paul passed through Lycaonia on all three of his recorded missionary journeys, visiting the cities of Derbe and Lystra. By the 1st century CE, Lycaonia was a Roman district in the region of Galatia, with Pamphylia and Cilicia to its south, Cappadocia to its east and Pisidia to its west. Some suggest this region may have been viewed as a less refined area by the time of Paul's visit, evidenced by the fact they were still speaking a local language (14:11). Paul and Barnabas crossed a frontier between Iconium and Lystra, a distance of about 20 miles. As an inland region the area may have been more difficult to Hellenize, for the region of Lycia spoke the Greek language by the 2nd century BCE.

The century before Paul's visit, the region had been much larger, but under Pompey's rule (64 BCE), part of it was given to Cappadocia, another to Cilicia, and yet another to Galatia. It wasn't until 25 BCE, the year King Amyntas died, that the southern and northern regions were then combined to form the Roman province of Galatia.

Timotheus (Timothy) lived in Lystra in Lycaonia. Paul met him there and took him along on his journey (16:1-3). Gaius, another traveling companion of Paul was also from Lycaonia, from the city of Derbe (20:4). Some scholars argue that the letter of Galatians was written to the believers in this area, than to ones in the northern region of Galatia because no travel by Paul to the northern region of Galatia is known.

Lycia (Region)

Acts 27:5 (Patara 21:1)

This mountainous region on the southern coast of Asia Minor (due northeast of the island of Rhodes) has a rocky shoreline along the Mediterranean. Paul visited this region twice: first, towards the end of his Third Missionary Journey as he sailed to Patara and took a boat from to Phenice; and later, after being arrested in Jerusalem, he was a prisoner that was moved from one ship to another at the port of Myra.

Lycian origins are uncertain, a matter of scholarly dispute. Clearly the Persians overtook them in 546 BCE, though they had in years past resisted the control of the legendary Lydian King Croesus. The Athenians ruled the area for a brief period during their "Classical Period" (468-446 BCE), and was lost again to the Persians for a time. They willingly came under the rule of Alexander the Great and by the 2nd century BCE, and eventually gave way to Roman expansion. During the time of Paul,

Claudius annexed to Pamphylia the area, and later Nero took this land and made it an independent district.

Lystra

Acts 14:8-19

In contrast to the larger and more prominent cities of the mission journeys of Paul, Lystra was a much smaller city. After the unwanted attention of the mobs of Iconium, Paul was perhaps looking for a safe haven in this young Roman colony, established in only 6 BCE. Though a Gentile and largely Latin speaking colony, the dialect was beyond the comprehension of Paul and Barnabas (Acts 14:11). Some scholars suggest that the team stayed in the home of Timothy during the visit on this journey (cp. Acts. 16:1).

When a cripple was healed and began to walk the crowd at Lystra began to venerate the Apostle and his companion, believing them to be gods in human form. After numerous attempts to persuade them otherwise, Paul eventually found a forum to preach to them. During the time of Paul's visit, some of the Jewish community of Antioch and Iconium began to stir the town against Paul. Eventually, the tide of public opinion turned, and they stoned Paul, leaving him for dead outside the city. The following day, Paul arose from the stoning and went southeast on to Derbe.

Macedonia (Region)

Acts 16:9

The ancient Kingdom of Macedonia is now part of Greece (comprising six regions of the eighteen regions of Greece today). The term was also used by General Tito I the twentieth century and applied to the (now named) country of Macedonia, but is a distinct region from the ancient reference. With well over one and one half million people, the area is 61 square kilometers, and is bordered to the south by the Aegean Sea. Abundant in small inlets, the major port is in Thessaloniki, where much of Eastern Europe imports and exports.

The area is subject to northern winds called the *vardaris winds*. Wind in the summer is generally northward off of the water. The area rainfall averages 190 mm. annually. Temperatures range from a high in July at +41.8C to a low in January −10.3C. The humidity ranges between 30 and 60%. In addition to shipping, the area yields some Cotton (50%), grain (35%), oats, barley and some vegetables.

Some scholars suggest that the Macedonian man may have been the Physician Luke, since it would be impossible to distinguish a Macedonian in a dream simply by appearance. In addition, the "we" sections begin (sections where Luke was apparently on the team) at the Macedonian mission (Acts 16:10-18, 20:5-16, 21:1-18, 27:1, 28:16).

After the vision, Paul came via Samothrace (the wind blew south to north). After one brief stop at the harbor of Samothrace, the boat traveled on to Neapolis. The two days of journey from Troas to Neapolis indicates the weather was good, and winds were favorable. (Later it would take five days near Troas, Acts 20:16). In the arrival, the Gospel came to what would one day be the edge of Europe, though Paul only saw it as another province of Rome. Perhaps Paul was determined to follow the Via Egnatia Road all the way to the Adriatic Passageway, on his way to Rome. This was interrupted by troubles in Thessalonica, which lead him to Berea, and eventually diverted him to Athens and Corinth.

Melita (Island of)

Acts 28:1

In spite of a few scholars that insist the location of Melita should be identified with Melitene (on the Dalmation coast), the vast majority of scholars favor the location of Paul's shipwreck as the island of Malta. This island is 100 kilometers (60 miles) south of Sicily, and due east of ancient Carthage in North Africa.

The island came under Roman rule in about 218 BCE as the Romans expanded south and controlled trade routes with Africa. This island was excellent haven for wintering ships due to its natural harbor. The island was about 18 miles long and though a bit arid it offered good building stone and on the east of the island - wool and olive oil. Melita enjoyed liberty as a free island and was able to run her own affairs. This island seemed to be a reasonably prosperous during the Roman period as a trade port.

The vessel that carried Paul and Luke was destroyed in a storm, torn in pieces probably in the area between the waters of the islet of Salmonetta and the west shore of the bay. Paul and his fellow prisoners wintered for three months.

On this island, the locals were hospitable (no doubt used to shipwrecks) and provided for the lost crew. Paul had opportunity to minister healing to the sick people of this island when he healed the father of Publius, a chief man of the island. Paul probably had a number of opportunities and preached the gospel. A flourishing church was established there according to later accounts. One tradition relates that Publius was the first believer I Jesus. After their stay, they left in an Alexandrian ship bound for Syracuse.

Miletus

Acts 20:16-38; Possibly 2 Tim. 4:20

The southern-most Ionian port, Miletus stood at the mouth of the Meander River. It had a long and glorious history. In the C8-C6 BCE it was strong enough a power to settle new colonies in areas as far away as the Black Sea, and maintained an important and profitable trade relationship with Egypt.

Famous personalities were associated with the city that was dubbed "the birthplace of Greek philosophy". The great "father of philosophy" named Thales lived in the city (640-546 BCE), and was followed by other important philosophers, such as the so-called "father of geography" Anaximander (611-547 BCE), Hecataeus the chronicler and Anaximenes (550-500 BCE). Pharoah Neco made an offering at the Milesian Temple after his victory at Megiddo and recapture of Carchemish (608 BCE, cp. 2 Kings 23:29; 2 Chron. 35:20). The offering did not help him from being overwhelmed a few years later by Nebuccanezzar II (605 BCE).

The Persians destroyed the original harbor in 495 BCE, and the whole area was reconstructed in 479 BCE. This new improved city suffered a crushing blow at the hands of Alexander the Great (334 BCE) during his campaign through the region. Rebuilt again, the city boasted four harbors and three agora (market) areas from the Hellenistic through Roman times (325 BCE to 325 CE).

The city was taken by Rome in 130 BCE, and somewhat redesigned. During Roman times, the harbor was silting slowly (now creating an inland lake five miles from the coast). This problem was causing constant problems and gradually forcing the city into an economic decline. Another market force also hurt the city. The major export was likely superior wool called "Milesia Vellera" which sold in markets in Rome and Alexandria in the early Roman period, but also declined when the Romans bred the variety in their homeland. A city of former glory, it experienced the decline that eventually befell Ephesus.

Paul visited the city some thirty five miles from Ephesus (a two day journey on foot), allowing some time for the Apostle to strengthen the Milesian faithful, and to prepare for a moving moment with his beloved disciples arriving from Ephesus. He loved them, but he dared not stop in Ephesus if he was going to keep to his vow to visit Jerusalem by Shavuot. His heart for them as he ended this Third Mission Journey is easily spotted in the record of the sermon (Acts 20:22ff).

Among the remains of the city is an impressive theatre that visitors can enjoy today. The original seated about 15,000 people. Found among the stones in the excavation between the third and sixth row of seats, was an inscription that read: "Place of the Jews, also called the God fearing".

Mitylene

Acts 20:14

Paul harbored overnight in the city as he traveled from Philippi down the western side of Asia Minor on his way to Jerusalem. The Third Mission Journey nearly complete, Paul stopped in Mitylene just before he made his way to the tear-filled address to the Ephesian elders at Miletus. Mitylene is a town situated on the eastern edge of the island of Lesbos a few kilometers off the coast of Western Asia Minor. (Though very close to the modern Turkish coast, the ancient Greek island is under the Greek flag today.) Its proximity to the old trade routes between the Hellespont and other ports to its south and east made it an important commercial and cultural center in ancient times.

Lesbos was and island colonized by the Aeolian Greeks who settled Mitylene before 1000 BC. By the 7th century Mitylene was culturally and commercially well established and eventually became part of the Athenian Empire. Sappho of Lesbos was a famous poetess that wrote emotional poetry of her female students that gave the appellation "lesbian" its current sense, though originally it was merely a reference to the emotional literature. The Greek island developed a sense of independence under the Romans and was noted by historians as a popular resort for Roman Aristocrats until an earthquake in 151 CE destroyed Mitylene. The city thrives today, and is still an exceptional place for a quiet vacation!

Myra

(Acts 27:5-6)

The city of Myra was a chief Lycian port in antiquity. Including both the city and the harbor a short distance away, the once prosperous city was near to the Lycian tombs (a short walk to the north), a rock carved necropolis with an impressive façade from the C4 BCE and onward. Along with the necropolis, there was a Roman theatre erected, which still appears in a good state of preservation. The port regularly serviced Alexandrian grain ships, serving the needs of the Lycian Cities. Though not extensively excavated, the city has significant remains

Julius the Centurion chose the ill-fated ship bound for Italy to take Paul for his requested presentation to Caesar (Acts 27:5-6). The contrary winds and waves eventually overwhelmed the vessel. Christianity took hold in the city, and a world famous Christian bishop of Myra. St. Nicolas is remembered in the restored C 11 CE Byzantine basilica. Nicolas was a late C4 CE bishop who served the people of his region with zeal, and is remembered as a particularly selfless and giving Christian. After a gift of three small bags of gold were left as dowry payments from three young women of Patara (to aid them in escaping a life of prostitution) the fame of his selfless acts grew in historical legend. It was said that Nicolas sold possessions dear to him to gain the money to care for these women. Today, a pawnbroker uses the three balls of gold to remember this gift. St. Nicolas is today the patron of Russia, virgins and sailors in liturgical settings, and is remembered world wide in the "Santa Claus" tradition.

Mysia (Region)

Acts 16:7,8

It seems Paul never traveled through the general area of Mysia though only on its outer borders. During his second journey, the Holy Spirit would not allow him to go into this region or Bithynia, so he went to Troas. On his third journey he traveled from Phrygia to Ephesus and then to Macedonia, but it is unknown whether he traveled through Mysia on his way to Macedonia. He could have, had he gone through Pergamum and Troas. Because at times Mysia's borders were not precisely defined, some wonder if these two cities (and Assos) were included in this region, for when Paul went to Troas he bypassed Mysia (16:8). It is thought that Troas was not only the name of a city, but was also of a geographical section of Mysia, as were Mysia Major, Mysia Minor, Aeolis, and Teuthrania.

Geographically, Mysia was located in the Northwest of Asia in what is now modern Turkey. To its north were the Hellespont (Dardanelles), the Sea of Marmora and Bithynia. Phrygia was to the southeast, Lydia was to its south, and the Aegean Sea was to the west.

In 133 BCE, Mysia was taken by Rome and was made a part of Asia when Attalus III bequeathed properties to Rome. Beforehand it had been included in the kingdom of Pergamum. The early settlers of this region were probably of Indo-European accent and settled here as invaders.

Neapolis

Acts 16:11

Following the vision of the Macedonian man Paul received at Troas, he journeyed to Neapolis (by way of the island of Samothrace). Of the "abundance of Revelations" Paul had received, we are only privy to three in significant detail: the vision into Heaven with words he "could not utter", the Macedonian man vision at Troas and the vision of the Risen Savior on the Damascus road. It may be that Luke joins Paul here at Neapolis, since the pronouns in the Book of Acts change from "them" to "we", suggesting the writer's personal presence in the events until Philippi. The two-day journey from Troas to Neapolis on the Second Mission Journey suggests the weather was good. The same journey took five days in less cooperative weather for the friends of Paul that were coming to see him in Troas from Philippi's port, which is Neapolis (cp. Acts 20:6).

Set against the slopes of Mt. Simvolo, the city of Kavalla appears as a great amphitheatre surrounding a concave harbor. The streets of the city rise up from the harbor into the mountainside. Though a city of more than one hundred thousand people, the place has a village feel. An important trade route of antiquity, this city still enjoys the prosperity as the center of a lucrative tobacco trade, and is set along a major east – west traffic route less than two hundred kilometers (170) from Thessaloniki. In the Roman period, the city acted as a port for the important Roman garrison at Philippi about fifteen kilometers away.

The history of the region is thought by local archaeologists to extend back to the Neolithic period. Nearby emergency excavations have revealed traces of a string of tiny ancient villages that appeared in the Classical Period (500-336 BCE). The city of Kavalla's history is best illustrated through a series of name changes over the centuries.

The oldest village was established between 3000 BCE and 500 BCE as a natural seaport, though scholars are uncertain of its ancient name. After 300 BCE, the village was rebuilt and referred to as "Neo-Porticus" perhaps due to some large stoas built as warehouses at the port. At least one source suggests that Philip II and his son Alexander the Great allowed the city become an "asylum" home for those who worked the Mt. Pangeo gold mines.

Roman control was extended to the city by 168 BCE. Before the Battle of Philippi in 42 BCE, the city was the station of Brutus and Casius. The primary purpose of the Roman city was to act as a port for the nearby garrison at Philippi, accessible only by a steep climb from the port over the western spur of Mt. Simvolo. After their defeat by Marc Antony and Octavian, the city was renamed "Neapolis" (new city) and held that name at the time of Paul's visit (Acts 16).

As a result of the message of Christianity taking hold in the region, the church grew in strength, and under the Byzantines the seat of the Bishop of Philippi was established there, with yet another name change to "Christopolis" (350 CE). References to the city throughout the period of Byzantine control refer to the city this way. Even the Crusaders (Franks) called the port "Christople".

With the rise of Ottoman control, the fourteenth century Ottomans renamed the port Cavallo, a vulgarization of Latin word "horse", perhaps because of use in postal service of Ottoman postal system. Some have suggested the name originally came from the shape of the peninsula in the place of the Old City. By the sixteenth century, the city had an essential role, as the flow of postal information to the Balkan holdings of the Ottomans was dependent on the key cities of the route. Sultan Sulieman "the Magnificent" added stability to the city by providing the impressive aqueduct that carried water from springs on the upper slope of Simvolo to the walled peninsula.

Inside the walled village of the Cavallo of the Ottoman Empire Muhammad Ali (1769-1849) was born. Ali was the Egyptian ruler of peasant revolt of 1805. As a result of the revolt, Muhammad Ali eventually broke with the Ottomans and established the last dynasty on the Egyptian throne that ended with King Fuad in 1953 (with the rise of Nasser).

Because of its position, the city bore the brunt of Greek - Turkish wars as the Ottoman Empire collapsed and the Balkans plunged into war at the time of the First World War. The town was occupied by Bulgarians, and eventually fell to German control by 1941. It was not until after World War II that the port was returned to Greece in late 1944. It now serves as the principal port for the export of tobacco, wheat, textiles and sugar beets. Its trading center is considered one of the most important for the continued strong economy of the Macedonia and Thrace regions.

The city has several important churches that attract visitors: the Church of St. Paul (established 1928); and the Church of St. Nicholas (formerly a church of St. Paul), which was converted to mosque under Ottoman occupation. All the churches had the desire to recall the "initiation of Christendom in Europe" in Paul's Second Mission Journey.

Beyond the churches, other historical sites of interest include: the "Old Quarter" named Panayia, after the Virgin Mary Church that once stood in the district on the peninsula area in the east of city. The fortress is from the early Paleologian Byzantine revival 13th CE. The former "Imaret" is one of the largest Muslim buildings in Europe (Kowa, "Bistro!"). Other important Ottoman buildings include the "House of Muhammed Ali" and the Kameres Aqueduct, built by Sulieman.

Pamphylia (Region)

Acts 2:10; 13:13; 14:24; 15:38; 27:5

Pamphylia, located in what is now modern day Turkey, was a coastal region that bordered the Mediterranean Sea to its south. The region was framed by Lycia to the southwest, Pisidia to the north and Cilicia to the east. The region had at least three main towns on its coastal: Attalia (today called Antalya) where Paul sailed from after visiting the region (14:25-26); Perga, a town a few miles east and somewhat inland with a river harbor; and Aspendos, used at one time by the Persians as a naval base before they were routed by the armies of Alexander.

During the period of the Diadoche (the successor generals of Alexander the Great), Ptolemy I and Ptolemy III of Egypt held this region for a brief period. Eventually the area was brought under Seleucid reign. The Romans took control of the region in the C2 BCE, and King Amyntas of Galatia received this area from Marc Antony in 36 BCE. Amyntas ruled there until he died in 25 BCE. A generation later, during the time of Paul's travels, Claudius (43 CE) took the region of Galatia and made it part of the province of Lycia-Pamphylia.

Paul visited the region of Pamphylia during his First Missionary Journey. In the Pamphylian city of Perga Paul preached (14:25) and the Book of Acts records John Mark, the nephew of Barnabas, left Paul and went back to Jerusalem (13:13; 15:38). The departure of John Mark led to a later break up in the relationship between Paul and Barnabas, as they could not agree on John Mark's readiness to endure hardship on a subsequent journey.

Paphos (Cyprus)

Acts 13:6-12

On the western shore of Cyprus, this city was the seat of the provincial administration and included a religious worship center dedicated to the worship of Aphrodite (Venus). Paphos was founded in the fourth century BCE over a previous site now referred to as "Palaipaphos" (ancient Paphos). By the end of the second century BCE it seems to have become the leading city of the island, but sustained real damage as a result of an earthquake in 15 BCE. After a period of reconstruction, the city celebrated a renewed status with several honors, including Emperor Augustus Caesar's conferred title "Augusta" given to the city, and later the extra title of "Claudia" (possibly conferred by Nero). Other scholar's suggest that Paphos' importance during Roman times can also be ascertained by the fact that milestones mark distances from it. It is no surprise that in this city Paul met the Proconsul of the island, Sergius Paulus.

Some scholars suggest that it was the former home of Barnabas, who was a Cypriot (Acts. 4:36). On the First Mission Journey, Paul and Barnabas witnessed the conversion of the

Proconsul Sergius Paulus. They also withstood the sorcerer Elymas in this city (Acts 13:9ff).

The nearby sanctuary of Apollo Hylates west of the city may have been developed in conjunction with a sanctuary and healing center of Asclepius at Citium (a nearby city with an excellent excavation that attracts visitors today), which was active at the time of Caesar Augustus. By the time of Paul, it is also possible that the sanctuary of Paphian Aphrodite also came to be linked to the imperial cult, though this is not universally accepted by scholars.

Patara

Acts 21:1-2

On the southern edge of Turkey in the Xanthus Valley, the ancient Mediterranean harbor of Patara was marked by a prominent hill that may have held a lighthouse. The port area is now silted and marshy, but the Patara of old was a famous city. The winter setting for the Oracle of Apollo each year, the city eventually rose to prominence and became the judicial seat of the Roman governor. The city was an outfitting and launching place for longer journeys, like a journey to Alexandria or Phoenician cities.

The remains of the city today include two Roman bathhouses, including one known as the "Baths of Vespasian" (69-79 CE). In addition, a theatre that is fairly well preserved (though partly filled with sand) and a Temple of the Corinthian order are discernible.

Alexandrian texts of Acts 21:1 state that Paul made his way to Tyre by means of Patara, but the Western text adds the "and Myra" that many scholars believe was a scribal error influenced by Acts 27:5-6. It is likely that the Alexandrian text reflects the original event, as the prevailing winds made Patara a better launch site for this long journey. Emperor Hadrian and his wife Sabina visited here (circa 130's CE), and a granary of Hadrian can still be seen west of the harbor marsh.

Perga

Acts 13:13

As the capitol of the region of Asia Minor called Pamphilylia, this city was served by the port of Attalia (today called Antalya) on the Mediterranean Sea. Just over five miles from the port, the city enjoyed the constant availability of products from both east and west, as well as the moderate climate of a Mediterranean city. The city rivaled Ephesus in its beauty (though a bit smaller) and celebrated its Greek culture in architecture and presentation. Paul and Barnabas arrived here along with Barnabas' nephew John Mark, who abandoned the team from here. This proved to be a point of contention that eventually divided Paul and Barnabas.

Phenicia (Region, also spelled Phoenicia)

Phenice: Acts 11:19; 15:3; Phenicia: 21:2; Tyre: 12:20; 21:3, 7; Sidon: 12:20

Phenice is the region of Phoenicia (also spelled "Phenicia" Acts 21:2) located on the eastern coast of the Mediterranean Sea. Its borders extended from Acco (modern Acre) in the south, northward to Mount Cassius, near the city of Arvad. Modern day Israel, Lebanon, and Syria are now located on its former domain. The area was about 185 miles long and probably no more than 20 miles wide. Phoenicia, derived from a Greek word, meaning "red purple" or "dark red" and was probably given because the natives used the Murex snails to produce dyes of this color. (Some scholars note another meaning for *phoinix* may have been "date-palm" as this tree has been found on Phoenician coins). Semites called this land part of "Canaan".

The Phoenicians, well known as expert sailors, established many trading posts throughout the Mediterranean, in Spain, Sicily and Africa's northern coast. It seems that many of this region took advantage of the sea, as there was limited farmlands on the narrow strip, though through earlier migration, seamanship also could have been brought from the Persian Gulf. The Phoenicians, like the Greeks, to whom they introduced the alphabet, focused their power on their cities and not outlying regions. Phoenicia's exact border was not certain, nor was the region itself consistently held under a strong political unit. The greatest Phoenician city was Sidon, and historically was usually teamed with Tyre, as was Acco with Dor.

Several schools of thought are evident on the subject of Phoenician origins. Some scholars note the Phoenicians were Semitic and migrated to the land from the "Fertile Crescent" and beyond, around the time of Abraham, 2000-1000 BCE. Others relate them more to the Sea Peoples of the Achaens region. By Jesus' time the Phoenicians bloodline might have been highly mixed with other cultures, especially Greek, as they had been ruled by and traded with other nations. The Phenice in Acts 27:12 is a port city of Crete, also known as Phoenix.

Philippi

Acts   16:12-40

Paul's trip into Macedonia brought him from the harbor at Neapolis, 9 miles (15 km.) northwest over the ridge to Philippi. This strategic Roman garrison city became the place of the first established church congregation, with early converts to Christianity. Philippi was located 115 miles northeast of Salonika (Thessaloniki), now close to the Bulgarian border. The city occupies the edge of a plain east of Mt. Pangaeus, tucked in the valley between the Lekani (east) and Phalakro and Menikio (north). Mt. Pangeo was the sacred mountain of Dionysos in antiquity, as well as the area of great gold and silver mines. The plain area had a large swampy valley in the ancient period, but the swamp was drained in the 1930's by a canal system for irrigation.

The city may have been the home of the Physician Luke who traveled with Paul on occasion. As a result, Luke may have taken special interest in his description of the city as the "capitol of first district of Macedonian Rome" (Acts. 16:12) a reference to the historical division of Macedonia earlier in the Roman period. In addition to its historical importance, Philippi was located along the important "Via Egnatia", the Roman road from Asia Minor that traversed the Balkan Peninsula toward the Adriatic Sea to ports with direct passage to Italy. In a sense, Philippi was the great roadway garrison station for the "eastern gate" from Europe to the Persian cities. By Roman times, the city had two types of citizens: Italians commissioned to live here and "political proselytes" like Paul and Silas, who were brought into the Roman citizenry by legislation of Rome.

Excavations of the city began when Napoleon Bonaparte (C18-19th) gave an imperial edict to French scholars to begin the archaeology at Philippi in the Forum where some buildings were already showing or close to the surface. After a long delay from the original excavations, they were renewed in 1914 under the auspices of the French Archaeological School working until 1937. Modern excavations have been undertaken by the Hellenic Archaeological Service, the Archeological Society of Athens, and the University of Thessaloniki.

Archaeologists have carefully constructed a working model of the occupation of the site. The earliest periods (Neolithic to Early Bronze) yield evidence of a settlement referred to as the "Dikli-tach", a group that used the flood plain for agriculture eventually gave way to a Thracian culture settlement. The city was founded as early as 700 BCE, and the site was well populated by both Thasos and the Thracian peoples during the Classical Period. The Classical period name of the site was **CRENIDES** (fountains), possibly because of a large ornament in the city square or the vast amount of surface water.

As King Philip II of Macedon took complete control of the region (365 BCE, control after 358/7 BCE) as a border garrison fort against Thrace, he swept in to dominate the nearby gold mines at Mt. Pangaeus. The gold was used to finance the build up of Philip's (and later Alexander's) army. With the rise of Rome, King Perseus (last of the Macedonian Kings) was routed from the Macedonian throne and ceded the area to Roman control. The Romans initially divided the area into four districts, later reorganizing Macedonia by 148 BCE as a single province.

Philippi became a Roman possession after Rome punished the Macedonian King Philip V for supporting the Carthaginians in the Punic Wars. The first defeat of the Macedonians was first in 197 BCE at Kynoskephalai, and a later at Pydna in 168 BCE. In the process, Philippi was devastated by the Roman army, and needed great restoration. The addition of the "Via Egnatia" military supply roadway put the city firmly on the map. The Via Egnatia passed (west to east) from Apollonia and Dyrrachium (in Albania) to Lychidnus, Herakleia Edhessa, Pella, Thessaloniki, Amphipolis and Philippi to Neapolis. After 46 CE it was extended to Byzantium (called later Constantinople).

The city became famous as a result of the Battle of Mark Antony and Octavian (later Augustus Caesar) against the conspirators and murderers of Julius Caesar, Brutus and Cassius (killers of Julius Caesar). The battle raged beside the city (largely in the swampy region to the west of the city. Philippi was commemorated by being granted colony status (an outpost for immigrants and warriors). Its new full name became "Colonia Augusta Julia Philippensus". This colony status offered four practical things to the citizenry: 1) full voting rights; 2) free trade with Rome; 3) guarantee of protection of Rome (i.e. "Bullmark of the Empire"); and 4) soldiers of defeated battles and armies lived here in clemency. When Mark Antony turned against Octavian in 31 BCE and fought at Actium (NW Greece), Octavian defeated him. Octavian became Caesar Augustus, and garrisoned Philippi substantially as the eastern buffer of Europe.

Luke apparently joins Paul, Silas and Timothy in Neapolis. Acts 16:12 records the arrival of the Gospel to Macedonia through Paul's Second Mission Journey. With no synagogue in the city, Paul goes to *proseuche* (a temporary place of prayer) to observe Sabbath. The stream off of the Gangites River (called the Zygakte River today) was the likely place where Paul came upon Lydia. The irony of the vision of the Macedonian man that brought Paul to Macedonia was that his first recorded convert was a Thyatiran saleswoman! (cp. Acts 16:4, 21-33). An inscription found in Philippi for her craft says the "city honors among the purple dyers, one Antiochus the son of Lyfos, a Thyatiran as a benefactor", an evidence that this trade was represented at Philippi.

Paul uses citizenship as protection (Acts 16:37-38). Later, Paul explains to the Philippian believers that their true "citizenship" is in Heaven in the letter written to them! The conversion of the Philippian jailer is another important story from the journey (Acts

16:21-33). Believers from this small church became important in Paul's ministry. This church became a chief financial supporter and Philippians 4:16 suggests that the epistle written to them by Paul was a "Thank You" letter for a financial gift! The trip of Epaphroditus to Paul was apparently the third support offering sent by them. With the town filled with soldiers and slaves, it is no wonder that Paul used language associated with the chariot racing language as "Press toward the prize".

The site today has yielded extensive evidence of worship of various pagan gods on reliefs, etc. found around the precipice of the city. These reliefs contain images such as Greek and Thracian gods, Eastern (Babylonian?) gods, and the Egyptian gods of Isis and Serapis. Harpocrates also had a shrine there. Above the city on the acropolis, one can still see remains of existing ramparts and citadel defenses. In addition, an impressive theatre built in C4th BCE and altered in C2nd CE is extant. A possible third alteration in C3 CE allowed the dramatic theatre to be transformed in purpose to a place for gladiatorial and beast contests.

The Roman forum is well represented, with fountains on both the east and west ends. A Roman lavatory and several later Basilicas are also evident. The bishopric of the Byzantine occupation is under excavation now.

Phrygia (Region)

Acts 2:10; 16:6; 18:23

Phrygia was a large and fertile inland province in Asia Minor, whose boundaries increased or decreased in different periods. At its largest it bordered the Black Sea, but most often it encompassed part of the valley of the upper Sangarius, as well as part of the Meander basin. In most periods the land extended from the area of Iconium to the north. This vast tract of land was part of an ancient kingdom attributed in legend to King Midas.

By the Roman Period, it was a highland plateau surrounded by Mysia, Lydia and Caria (westward), Bithynia (to the north), Pisidia, Lycia, and Isaura (to the south) and Lycaonia (eastward). Some of these provinces were included in historical references as part of Phrygia (at times Pisidia) as the term was used as a general regional description in some sources. Iconium was considered the capital of Phrygia. Other important cities that are mentioned in the Book of Acts include Laodicea, Heirapolis, Colossae and Antioch of Pisidia. The cult of Cybele apparently originated here (see article on Ephesus) and became quite fashionable among some Romans of the wealthier classes.

Excavations of the cities of Phrygia reveal a large and prosperous economy, due in part to the rich pastureland for both sheep and cattle. The province was also mineral rich. The Asian province came under Roman control beginning in 133 BCE. By 116, all the territory was Roman, and the easternmost portion was put in the hands of the new "Phrygia-Galatica" provincial governor.

Jewish people of Babylon and Mesopotamia were settled in Phrygia by Antiochus the Great. These Jews were referred to in some sources as less austere in the keeping of their faith, and were accused of mixing comfortably with the practices of the around them, though some did attend feasts in Jerusalem (Acts 2:10). Phrygia was well populated in the period with an excellent road network accessible for industry and trade. Phrygia was well known for its textile products and for horses bred for the Roman circus.

Devout Jews from Phrygia formed part of the crowd of people in Jerusalem who heard the preaching of the gospel at Pentecost from Peter and the other apostles (Acts 2:10). They may have been the first to form churches in Phrygia (Acts 2:41). The apostle Paul entered Phrygia with Barnabas at Antioch of Pisidia. Paul was given opportunity to speak and received a great response from both Jews and Gentiles. On the next Sabbath "came almost the whole city together to hear the word of God" (Acts 13:44). Sadly, some unbelieving Jews stirred up trouble and had them cast out of the area. He and Barnabas returned later to Iconium to strengthen and confirm the believers (Acts 14:32).

On a second trip with Silas and Timothy, Paul returned and went throughout Phrygia to see how the brethren were doing also giving them the instruction from the Apostles and elders in

Jerusalem (Acts 15:36,40; 16:1-4,6). Paul went throughout all Phrygia and Galatia on a third journey "strengthening all the disciples" on his way to Jerusalem where he determined to celebrate the Feast (Acts 18:23).

Pisidia (Region)

Pisidia: Acts 13:14; 14:24. Pisidian Antioch in 13:14; 14:19,21; 2 Timothy 3:11

Pisidia was a province located in south central Asia Minor, tucked on the northern rim of the Taurus mountain chain and due south of Galatia proper. It was bordered by Pamphylia and Lycia to its south, Lycaonia to its east. Paul probably passed through the region on all three of his missionary journeys. Pisidian Antioch, the province's greatest city, was founded by the Seleucids and was named to distinguish it not from the Syrian city by that name, but from the closer Antioch of Phrygia.

King Amyntas began his reign there in 36 BCE and ruled this mountainous region. He attempted to establish a colony at Antioch in 25 BCE, but died that same year in battles against the region's hill tribes. Neither the Persians nor the Greeks could overtake the lawless mountaineers of the nearby Taurus range. Pisidia had a larger population than the coastal regions, mainly because of the city of Antioch.

Paul visited this city at least twice during his missionary journeys and when he visited the area of Phrygia and Galatia (Acts 16:6; 18:23), it seems he might have also visited the believers here in Pisidia. Because Pisidian Antioch was easily accessible, had a local synagogue, this made a good environment in which Paul and Barnabas could spread the Gospel.

Ptolemais

Acts 21:7; Judges 1:31,32

Ptolemais (also called Acco, Acre and Akko in various periods) was an ancient Biblical city situated between Carmel and Tyre on the coasts of the Mediterranean Sea. Once a Canaanite (Phoenician) city, the land was allotted to the tribal territory of

Asher. Remains of that city are located at Tell el-Fukhkhar. The sandy beach south of the city was traditionally known for exceptional material for making glass. The shore north is rocky and rugged to the water's edge.

Ptolemais was an important Phoenician city in the Middle and Late Bronze Ages. Documented by Egyptians, Pharaoh Seti I of the 19th dynasty of Egypt landed near there on his first expedition to Canaan. The city was also apparently conquered (according to Egyptian accounts) before or during the reign of Pharoah Ramses II.

In the Iron Age, the tribe of Asher was unable to drive out the inhabitants of the city (Acco), but dwelt among the Canaanites (Judges 1:31,32). Acco came under Israelite control during the reign of King David. Much later, when Sennacherib of Assyria destroyed the northern Kingdom of Israel (701 BCE) Acco also suffered destruction. The city was reconstructed, and became an important mint and metalwork center by the time of Alexander's march to cut off any port access to the Persian navy (333-323 BCE). Acco was renamed Ptolemais in honor of Egyptian ruler Ptolemy II (during the period of the Greek rule in Egypt of the 4th century BCE). Roman soldiers were stationed in the city and Julius Caesar stopped there in 48 BCE. The port flourished in Roman times.

In 52-54 CE, Ptolemais was made a Roman colony and an influx of Romans settled the region. This city so flourished under paganism of the Greek and Roman periods, it was disputed over by Jewish rabbis as to whether it should be considered part of Israel or not. In the Book of Acts, there was apparently a Messianic community made up of Jews who had turned to Jesus probably through the preaching of those who had been scattered at the time of the persecution that arose from the death of Stephen (Acts 11:19). Paul stopped over for one day during his "Third Mission Journey", traveling between Tyre and Caesarea (Acts 21:7).

Although the Crusaders were unable to conquer Acco in their initial battles, the city was eventually defeated by King Baldwin in 1104. During the Crusader era there was a constant stream of merchandise and travelers in and out of Acco all year round as the city took on vast importance. Evidence of its greatness can be seen today in fabulous Crusader halls discovered during late 20th-century excavations. At this time of grandeur, Acco received yet another new name – this time it became known as St. Jean d'Acre. Over 3,000 years later, Acco's impressive walls proved to be the demise of a foreign army when Napoleon Bonaparte was forced to abandon his siege of the city with his troops. Acco became part of the British Mandate in 1922, and imprisoned Jews who fought the British are still remembered in a museum building (former prison) where they were once held prisoners.

Puteoli

Acts 28:13

This town is located on the Bay of Naples north of Pompeii in Italy. Puteoli (modern Pozzuoli) means "little wells" in Latin, and was established as a Samian Colony from Cumae in the 6th century BCE. The port was located opposite the island of Ischia, which kept its waters somewhat calmer than other exposed Western Italian ports. It is likely the city fell into Roman hands at the time of the conquest of Capua (338 BCE). According to Livy, there were 6,000 foot soldiers garrisoned there by the time of the first Carthaginian invasion (24.13). He also makes reference to large vessels bound for Spain with reinforcement troops.

The historian Josephus also mentions the town as one he visited (*Life* 3. Also, *Antiq.* xvii. 12, 1; xviii. 7, 2; *Wars* II, vii, 1). The traffic in the port apparently also included the grains and cotton of Egypt. Seneca reported the grain arrival from Alexandria passed through the port at Puteoli. The Via Domitiana roadway link leading from the city to the Via Appia gave support to the town as a major shipping center.

On his journey to Rome, Paul landed on shore at Puteoli and found fellow believers in Jesus there. Some scholars accept the recent find of the Byzantine period chapel in Herculaneum a likely marker for the home of Paul's visit. (Other excavations in the area include a well-preserved Flavian amphitheatre.) It appears took a barge from Puteoli via the Pontine Marshes to the Appii forum, though he may have traveled to Capua and then took the Appian Way to Appii forum (Acts 28:15).

It seems the Alexandrian ship (Acts 27:6) Paul was originally sailing on possibly had a grain shipment (27:38) and was therefore headed to Puteoli. "At this time Puteoli was the regular port of entry of Rome from the East, especially for large grain ships. Rome's own port, Ostia, was about this time being dredged to admit large ships, and thereafter largely supplanted the maritime importance of Puteoli." (Unger, *Archaeology and the New Testament*, Zondervan, p. 313).

It is no surprise that though Paul had never been to the Italian provinces and yet he met with believers in Puteoli (Acts 28:13-14). He was greeted by believers from Rome at two towns along the way to Rome (Acts 28:15), for in his letter to the Romans he mentions many by name (16:3-15).

Rhegium

Acts 28:13

Historians report Rhegium was established in 712 BCE. The city (today called Reggio di Calabria) was settled as a Greek colony on the southern tip of Italy set across from Messina in Sicily, and guarded the eastern bank of the Strait of Messina. This strategic harbor was a place of refuge for seafarers. The straight is approximately six miles wide and contained two obstacles for ships: the rock of Scylla and the whirlpool of Charybdis. Because of these difficult waters, a ship could rest at Rhegium until a good southern wind came to take it steadily through the straight, then further northward. This was one reason Rhegium was valued by Rome as it assisted further traveling to western Italy. At the time of Paul, ships from the east to contact with Rome most commonly used the port at Puteoli, which was north of Rhegium.

Rhodes (City and Island name)

Acts 21:1

The largest island of the Dodecanese (48 miles long, 23 miles wide) houses nearly 100,000 inhabitants today (and scores of tourists). Rhodes (or Rodos) has become the regional capital of the Dodecanese islands. The highest point of the island is Mt. Ataviros (at 125 m ASL) in the center of the island. The island is fertile with a great variety of vegetation. In antiquity the island bore 11 different names, among them: Aithraia, Ophiousa and Telchinis. The capital, also called Rhodos, occupies the northernmost tip of the island.

Rhodes (probably form "rose" in Greek) has a long and important history. The island was first inhabited in the Neolithic era. During the Bronze Age (3000-1150 BCE) three early cities were formed on the island: Kamiros (west), Lindos (east) and Ialysos (Near Filermos in north, not far from Rhodos city). The wares have been discovered at excavations in both Egypt and Italy. The island traded gold jewelry and ceramics decorated with oriental motifs or plants and animals in stylised form. Through the Greek Dark Age (1150-800 BCE) Rhodes was recalled in mythology (Pindar in one of his Odes) as the island of Helios (the sun god) - born of the union of Helios the sun god and the nymph Rhodia. By the Archaic Period (800-500 BCE) the Dorian invasion caused displacement of people groups in the Aegean. Rhodes was included in the formation (700 BCE) of the "Dorian Hexapolis" a union of cities with Knidos, Halikarnassos and Kos. It was home to Epimenedes the poet (600 BCE).

During the Classical Period (500-336 BCE) the Persians occupied the island for a brief time, but the Admiral Mentalos of Rhodes eventually routed them. In 408 BCE, the three chief cities of the island founded Rhodos city, which quickly outgrew them. The city was built under the plan of Hippodamos of Miletus and the league was wisely administered under tyrants, and prosperity increased, for a time finding themselves under Spartan rule.

In the period of Alexander and Diadoche (336-43 BCE) the rising tensions in the region forced great investment into a maritime fleet and produced protection and far-reaching prosperity. Rhodes was independent from 327 BCE when the Macedonian guard was removed and concentrated on an effective port, maritime law, and rescue service on the seas. A school of sculpture was developed and exported works abroad (Colossus of Rhodes* by Chares of Lindos – one of the seven "wonders of the world"; the "victory of Samothrace by Pythekritos; and Laocoon – now in the Vatican). The island was attacked in 304 BCE unsuccessfully, but had to recover from an earthquake in 277 BCE. By 200 BCE, it was a regular stop for the Roman fleet. [*The Colossus was probably built at 100 to 150 feet high in 302-290 BCE, but fell into the harbor during an earthquake in about 226 BCE, and was finally scrapped in 657 CE.]

The Roman Period (43 BCE-300 CE) brought destruction and reconstruction. Rhodes was not always constant in its loyalty to Rome. When opposed Rome, Rome retaliated by offering additional funding to Delos as a port (166 BCE) giving mainland Caria and Lycia an alternative port for trade. This crushed Rhodes economically and forced her to ally herself to Rome. In one raid, Gaius Cassius captured and laid waste to the city of Rhodes (now the capital). Paul harbored there (though most believe at Lindos) in about 57 CE (Acts 21:1). There is no record of any missionary work by Paul on this island. By that time Rhodes had diminished considerably to a small port but retained its beauty and marks of former prosperity as well as some important schools. Great Roman students taught on the island included Cicero, Lucretius, Julius Caesar, Tiberius Caesar and Marc Antony. Diocletian declared it a province in 297 CE.

Much later, the Crusader Period (1000-1450 CE) brought a period of stability (and building) to the island. In 1309 it fell into the hands of the Knights of St. John and became again a maritime power - symbolized by its magnificent medieval town and castle with the Palace of the Grand Masters. This period lasted until the fall under Sulieman II in 1522 CE. The buildings of the period mimic the buildings of Avignon, France. Likely this period also saw the creation of the Rhodes faience (brilliant enamels on ceramic plates probably originated in Lindos – or borrowed technology from Nicea).

In the Modern Period (1830-present) the island was taken in 1911 by the Italians (from the Turks) and they annexed it to protect the route to African colonies. They were responsible for much of the restoration on the island seen today. It was occupied by Germans from 1943-45, taken by the British, and made part of Greece on 7 March 1948.

Rome

Acts 2:10; 18:2; 19:21; 23:11; 28:14,16;Romans 1:7,15; II Timothy 1:17;

The date of the founding of Rome has been a debate among scholars for centuries. The classical date of 753 BCE is the most common, and is referred to as the beginning of the early monarchy (753-510 BCE). The legendary Romulus may have established been responsible for gathering the early villagers to a small fort some 24 kilometers from the Tiber River. Eventually the city engulfed eight hills: Quirinal, Caelian, Palatine, Aventine, Viminal, Esquiline, Oppian and Capital.

Rome had many advantages in its location. It was near the sea trade route of the Adriatic, and central to the Italian peninsula. The Italian peninsula was guarded by the Alps to the North and by the sea all around. The city benefited from the colonization of the Greeks, founding cities like Cumea, and hence bringing advanced civilization to the country (much of its reading, writing and religion derived from Greek mythology and philosophy).

Where the Greeks settled to the south of Italy, the Etruscans lived to the north. Etruria was predominantly an urban society, drawing wealth from the shipping trade, and was often depicted by the Romans to be a decadent and weak culture. While maintaining unique features, the Etruscans too had borrowed culture from the Greeks. Around 650 BCE the Etruscans crossed the Tiber and occupied Latium. As a result, scholars surmise the settlement on the Palatine Hill was brought together with the settlements on surrounding hills, either in an attempt to fend off the invaders, or, once conquered, by the Etruscan masters. At this point the first Kings appear.

Knowledge of early Rome is based primarily on two sources of evidence: the traditional histories written by Livy, Diodorus, and Plutarch (several centuries later); and the findings of archaeology. Legend says that the Romans traced their ancestry back to Aeneas, the hero who escaped from the sack of Troy carrying his father Anchises on his back. Later on Aeneas' son then founded the city of Alba Londa, and it was from the kings of Alba Longa that the legendary Romulus and Remus, the founders of Rome, were directly descended. The story of Romulus and Remus founding the city of Rome may incorporate elements of truth, for it was in the 8th century that two existing settlements, on the Palatine Hill, the other on the Quirinal, coalesced to form a single village. This was the approximate time that the traditional foundation of Rome by Romulus in 753 BCE.

From Village to City –Four Early Kings (c. 753-616 BCE)
The four earliest kings were shadowy characters and the settlement itself was small and undistinguished. Major change began to take place during the C7th BCE, when tiled roofs and stone foundations appear, culminating in the draining of the Forum area and its laying out as a public square. The first four rulers were indigenes tribal rulers, and are thought to have been:

1. Romulus (probably mythical): to him is attributed the founding, the extension to four of the Roman hill, - the Capitoline, Aventine, Caelian and Quirinal - and the infamous rape of the Sabine women.

2. Numa Pompilius: owing to the influence of his adviser, the nymph and prophetess Egeria, enjoyed a peaceful reign.

3. Tullius Hositilius: responsible for the destruction of Alba Longa and the removal of its inhabitants to Rome. With the destruction of this opponent they took over the sacred festivals of Latium and all the regional prestige and status that came with it.

4. Ancus Marcius: extended the city further, built the first bridge across the across the Tiber and founded Ostia at the mouth of that river to serve Rome as a seaport as a symbol of the city's increasing power.

An Etruscan Vassal City (c. 616-510 BCE)
After the period of the early monarchy, Rome was controlled by Etruscan leaders and took on many Etruscan trappings. They had established a major zone of influence in Campania (near Naples) to the south, and the Tiber Bridge was the strategic artery of communication between the homeland and these southern outposts. The Etruscans ruled Rome for a little over a

century until the eventual expulsion of Tarquinius Superbus (Tarquin the Proud) - probably over moral impropriety.

5. Tarquinius Priscus: an Etruscan, he mysteriously secured his kingship and continued the work of conquest, but found time to build the first sewer, the Cloaca Maxima, laid out the Circus Maximus, and began to erect on the Capitoline Hill a great temple to Jupiter. According to legend he took control of Rome by peaceful means, gaining the support of the leading families.

6. Servius Tullius: a celebrated monarch of great achievements. He divided the people into tribes and classes, setting up a constitution in which wealth was the dominant consideration. He is believed to have enlarged the city by building a wall around it, five miles in circumference with nineteen gates, embracing all the Seven Hills of Rome. He transferred the regional festival of Diana from Aricia to the Aventine Hill of Rome. Shortly afterwards a massive temple of ca. 60 meters length and 50 width (begun by Tarquinius Priscus) was dedicated on the Capitoline Hill to Jupiter.

7. Tarquinius Superbus (Tarquin the Proud): continued with great vigor the work of extending the power of the city, and the founding of colonies by him was the beginning of Rome's path to supremacy of the world. He irritated the people by the burdens he placed upon them. Eventually, his son Sextus outraged Lucretia (the wife of a prominent Roman), and Tarquinius was exiled by a group lead by a rich citizen named Brutus whose father's property he had seized. It is possible that this revolt was part of a larger rebellion by several Latin cities (Antium, Aricia and Tusculum) against a foreign Etruscan King. However, Tarquinus was not killed in the revolt and escaped to the Etruscans, on whose help he could count.

The Etruscan domination brought some long lasting effects to the Romans including the monetary system, building and architectural styles, and some religious traditions.

The Early Republic (510-450 BCE)

Livy recorded that the end of the Etruscan dynasties was brought about by the rape of Lucretia by prince Sextus, son of king Tarquin the Proud. The rape gave cause to Roman aristocrats led by Lucious Junius Brutus to incite rebellion. The Tarquins were expelled from Rome and a new constitution was devised, with power in the hands of the senate, who delegated executive action to a pair of consuls who were elected from among their number to serve for one year, thereby forming the Roman Republic. Rome for some time lay under the continued threat of Etruscan intervention, but Rome had won its independence. The idea of the Republic became an icon in later days, the honor of which all future leaders would have to publicly ascribe.

After some years of conflict the plebeians forced the senate to pass a written series of laws (the Twelve Tables), which recognized certain rights and gave the plebeians their own representatives, the tribunes. It was only much later (in the 4th century) that plebeians were given the right to stand for the consulship and other major offices of state.

Roman Expansions in Italy (450-270 BCE)

By 450 BCE, Rome was an important city, but no major regional power. The transition came by territorial expansion through a series of minor wars. By 400 BCE tribal peoples of the region had been defeated, and the Romans pushed forward their own frontiers, establishing colonies in strategic places.

First came the expansion through the battle of the Etruscan city named Veii: This represented the first resounding Roman military (**406-396 BCE)** after a ten-year siege. Veii was the southernmost of the Etruscan cities and a major metropolis. Next there was a time of delay in their expansions, as the Celtic Wars drew all Roman resources. In about **390 BCE**, the Celts (from Central Europe) sacked Rome and established themselves in northern Italy. They defeated the Romans at the River Allia and captured the city. The citadel on the Capitoline Hill held out for a few months but eventually capitulated. After they sacked the city, the Celts withdrew with their booty back in northern Italy, leaving the Romans to pick up the pieces, rebuild the city and restore their damaged prestige. In response, Rome rebuilt with better defenses: the Servian Wall, 6 miles (10 km) long, (the only city wall that Rome possessed until the Emperor Aurelian build a new one over 500 years later). It was some years before the Romans were able to return to the offensive.

In **343 BCE** Rome came into conflict with the Samnites, a powerful tribal confederation who controlled the central backbone of southern Italy. This First Samnite War was brief and inconclusive, but was followed by more significant Roman gains in the Second and Third Wars. The Third Samnite War extended Roman territory across the Apennines to the Adriatic Sea. This made Rome a major regional power and attracted hostile attention from the Greek cities around the coast of southern Italy. They called in the help of Pyrrhus, king of Epirus, an ambitious adventurer who arrived at Tarentum in 280 BC with a well-trained army which included war elephants, the first the Romans had encountered in battle.

The eastern Mediterranean World was being taken and controlled by the march of Alexander and his armies, followed by the period of the Diadoche. During this time, Rome was afforded the opportunity to grow unchecked in the west, and set it's sights on the Carthaginian control of the western and central Mediterranean.

Roman Expansion around the Mediterranean (270-130 BCE)

With the eastern Mediterranean struggling in wars between the Diadoche dynasties, more skirmishes made it possible for Rome to control virtually the whole of the Italian peninsula, either through alliance or direct conquest. Turning to the Carthaginians (Carthage was a maritime power) and the west and central Mediterranean, the Punic Wars fought for control of the region.

The First Punic War (264-41 BCE) was fought for control of Sicily. The Carthaginians had long held the western end of the island and had sought from time to time to conquer the Greek cities of eastern Sicily, such as Catana and Syracuse. Romans learned the naval tactic quickly, and defeated the Carthaginians. By the end of war Sicily was reduced to the status of a Roman province, becoming indeed Rome's first overseas possession. In the Second Punic War (218-202 BCE), the Carthaginians were slow to accept their earlier losses and in struck back with an invasion of Italy itself led by Hannibal. This time it was a land battle. The Romans turned the tables by invading Carthaginian territory. Hannibal crossed back to Africa to defend his homeland but was defeated in the battle of Zama the final battle of this war, by the Roman general Scipio Africanus. Essentially, The Third Punic War (160-146 BCE) served to eventually destroy Carthage, a major city-state in North Africa. The ground of Carthage was said to have been laid with salt in order to prevent the redevelopment of agriculture.

With the victory over Carthage, Rome awoke other enemies further afield. In the west, they became involved in a whole succession of wars in Spain, seeking to protect and expand the territory in the south of the country that they had taken from the Carthaginians. In Italy, close to home, they renewed the conquest of the Celtic lands in the north, which became the province of Gallia Cisalpina. The Romans declared war on Philip V, the king of Macedonia, because he backed Hannibal in the Second Punic War. In 196 BCE defeated the Macedonian army at Cynoscephalae. In 146 BCE (the year the Third Punic War ended), Rome forced Greece and Macedonia together to become the Roman province of Achaea. In 133BCE Rome gained territory when the last king of Pergamum left his kingdom to the Romans upon his death. The Aegean provinces brought wealth to Italy, and fortunes were made through the granting of valuable mineral concession and enormous slave run estates.

The Rise of "Champions of the Republic" (130-62 BCE)

The beginning of the end of the Republic came when the brothers Gracchus challenged the traditional constitutional order in the 130s - 120s BCE by land reform. Though members of the aristocracy themselves, they sought to parcel out public land to the dispossessed Italian peasant farmers. Other measures followed, but many senators came to view the Gracchi as public enemies, and both the brothers met violent deaths. A series of "Social Wars" were fought internally.

Other champions gained popularity, like Gaius Marius, a brilliant military commander who reformed the Roman army and saved Italy from the invading Cimbri and Teutones in 102 and 101 BC.

This phenomenon continued and was eclipsed by that of Sulla in the 80s BCE. Sulla made his name in two crucial wars. The first in Italy itself, the so-called Social War of 91-89 BCE, where the Italian allies, though they lost the war, largely won their demand for full Roman citizenship. The second was being the defeat of Mithridates, king of Pontus, who chose this moment of Roman weakness to overrun Asia Minor and Greece. Sulla was a staunch proponent of aristocratic privilege, and his short-lived monarchy saw the repeal of pro-popular legislation and the condemnation, usually without trial, of thousands of his enemies. Sulla attacked Athens and destroyed or pillaged it (86 BCE).

After Sulla's death the pendulum swung back somewhat in favor of the people under a successful new commander, Gneaus Pompey the Great. He became immensely popular for clearing the seas of pirates and he helped to defeat Spartacus during the slave uprisings. He went on to impose a new political settlement on the warring kingdoms of the east Mediterranean, notably making Syria a Roman province. When he returned to Rome in 62 BCE, he found himself faced by two astute political opponents: the immensely wealth Marcus Licinius Crassus, and the young but promising Gaius Julius Caesar.

The Triumvirate Accommodations (62-27 BCE)

The First Triumvirate: The three men Gnaeus Pompey, Marcus Licinius Crassus, and Gaius Julius Caesar reached a political accommodation on the terms of influence. Under the terms of this arrangement Caesar become consul in 59 BCE and was then made governor of the two Gallic provinces, Cisalpina south of the Alps, the other Transalpina covering the southern part of modern France. Rising in power, Caesar and Pompey eventually came to raising internal armies against one another in a Civil War (49-48 BCE) eventually won by Caesar at Pharsalus and chased Pompey to Egypt, where he was presented with Pompey's head (48). It is this venture to Egypt that introduced Cleopatra to Julius Caesar.

Julius Caesar's rising and popular career was cut short by his assassination at Rome in 44 BCE, but rule by one man was becoming an increasingly inevitable prospect. It was a prospect brought to fruition by Octavian, Caesar's adopted son. He and

Mark Antony (Caesar's friend and lieutenant) defeated Caesar's assassins at the Battle of Philippi in 42 BC.

The Second Triumvirate was formed when Octavian, Antony and Lepidus divided power between them. The arrangement did not last, however, and eventually resolved itself into direct military conflict between Octavian and Mark Antony. Octavian's victory at the Battle of Actium (31 BCE) left him sole ruler, and in 27 BC the Senate granted him the title Augustus, making him the first official emperor of Rome.

The Rise of The Great Empire (31 BCE)

Thus Rome grew from the period of the monarchy to the period of the great republic (510-31 BCE), a time that was forever recalled as a "Golden Era" by later poets and historians. The Republic gave way to the most powerful empire the world had ever known, as the Romans swept over the remains of the Greek expansions to the east. Though the technical Roman Empire began with Augustus Caesar, the seeds of single rulership and hero popularity had long been established. Augustus adorned Rome as the capital of the Roman Empire. Extravagantly constructed, the city had a senate and a temple in honor of Caesar, and an infamous Coliseum for games. The greatest part of the population lived in the valleys multiple family units that filled the area. The wealthy lived in large villas that were in themselves pieces of art, set in the surrounding hills. Rome provided her people with food, free games and entertainment in theaters and cheap wine.

The Romans were eclectic in religious tradition, and accepted a variety of Greek and eastern practices. Often Rome was given to great excesses and abuses, a symbol of immorality, idolatry, paganism and human decay as a world-ruling city, where emperor worship was a mandate.

Judea and Jerusalem came under Roman rule (led by Pompeii) in 63 BCE. The Roman political environment dominated at the time of Jesus and the early Messianic movement. Jesus was born during the rule of Augustus Caesar and ministered at the time of Tiberias Caesar. The story in the Book of Acts began in

Jerusalem (part of the Judean Province) and ended in the proclamation of the Gospel in Rome.

The founding of the Roman church is not known, but may have begun with Messianic Jews who were present on the day of Pentecost in Jerusalem after the preaching of Peter (Acts 2:10). There were probably also Gentile believers in the fellowship depicted in Paul's Epistle to the Romans (which apparently carried both references to the Jews and Gentiles - Romans 16:3-16). The letter to Rome was sent before Paul ever visited the city and there is no mention of the other apostles visiting Rome. Paul indicated his desire to visit the believers and preach to them (Acts 19:21; Romans 1:10-15) he arrived in Rome as a prisoner. Roman believers came out to meet Paul at the Appii Forum before he reached the city (Acts 28:14-16), as the movement had already taken hold in the region.

Paul was allowed to have visitors and continued to teach for a period of two years (Acts 25:12; 27:1; 28:19-31). Still in confinement in Rome, Paul referred to believers (whose nationality is not clear) in his letter to the Philippians as "of the household of Caesar" (Philippians 4:22). In his Second Epistle to Timothy, Paul referred to Onesiphorus who refreshed him in his chains in Rome (II Timothy 1:16-17).

Order and procedure in Roman law was evident in the record of Paul's interaction with authority. Roman citizenship protected Paul from mob justice as well as Roman scourging (Acts 16:35-39; 22:22-29).

Extensive persecution of followers of Jesus was first known under Emperor Nero (54-68 CE). When Paul appealed to Caesar, it may have been to Nero (Acts 25:11). Later, Paul was reportedly martyred (along with Peter and many others) under the same emperor (c. 67 CE) in Rome. From that time, persecution of Christians periodically occurred in "waves" as it became politically advantageous (i.e. they greatly increased during Domitian 81-96). The Apostle John's imprisonment to the island of Patmos can be related to Domitian (Revelations 1:9). This persecution worsened until the Edict of Milan in 313 that afforded Christianity the status "religion licita" (legitimate religion) in the Roman Empire.

Salamis

Acts 13:4-5

On the eastern coast of the island of Cyprus, Salamis may have been established after the time of Paphos (a rival city on the west side of the island), but eventually became more prominent. The harbor was a noted commercial center, providing timber for shipbuilding and copper that was exported from the inland mountain regions. The community was diverse, including enough Jews to have more than one synagogue, though the actual number is uncertain.

Salmone

Acts 27:7

Salmone was a cape on the northeastern extremity of Crete (now known as Cape Sidero). Salmone was an important landmark in Luke's account of the journey to Rome. The decision to sail on the south side of the island was apparently taken because of the wind direction at the time, with the sailors hoping to gain some shelter provided by the island. After passing Salmone, the ship continued west parallel to the southern shore of Crete toward Fair Havens.

Samaria (Region)

Acts 1:8; 8:1,5,9,14,25; 9:31; 15:3; 8; 1 Kings 13:32; 16:24,28,29,32; 2 Kings 1:2,3; 2:25; 7:1,18; 13:1,6,9,10,13; 23:18,19; Ezra 4:10,17; Nehemiah 4:2; Isaiah 7:9; 8:4; 19:9; Jeremiah 23:13; 31:5; Ezekiel 16:46; 23:4,33; Hosea 7:1; Amos 3:9,12; 4:1; 6:1; Obadiah 19; Micah 1:1; Luke 17:11; John 4:4,5,7,9.

The geographical region north of the hills of Jerusalem, between the Jordan rift valley and the Sharon coastal plain is known as Samaria. In the Biblical account, the territory was conquered by Joshua (Joshua 4-10). It had a number of important mountainous sites: Mt. Ebal and Mt. Gerizim in the central area and Mt. Carmel and Mt. Gilboa to the extreme north of the region. Samaria's southern boundary reached the road from Bethel in the central ridge, east to Jericho (the Wadi Auja pass today). The southern border (west) followed the valley of Aijalon to the Mediterranean. This area was the heart of the Promised Land, and several important Biblical stories were set in the mountains and valleys of Samaria.

The Bible contains a number of important records for events from within the region. Infamous for the unusual revenge taken after the rape of Dinah (Genesis 34), the Biblical city of Shechem was dominated by the mountains of Mt. Gerizim and Mt. Ebal. Some time later, the area of Mt. Gerizim included the renewal of the Covenant of the Tribes of Israel under the leadership of Joshua. After the conquest of this region under Joshua, it was inhabited by the tribes of Ephraim, Manasseh and Issachar. With the break-up of the United Kingdom of Israel, the northern tribes seceded from the tribal confederation and formed a northern kingdom that took the name "Israel" (as distinguished from the southern tribal name "Judah). Large cities of the central Samaria became centers for the new Israel, and new worship shrines were erected.

From this period some sixty-five *ostraca* (pieces of broken pottery upon which business transactions were written) have been found, receipts for the payment of taxes to Samaria. From sources such as these archaeologists provide a glimpse at the names of the payers and collectors of this ancient kingdom. In addition, the taxation was with produce rather than money and demonstrates a once vibrant barter economy. The region's fertile land and roads made it an adequate trading partner with neighboring nations (especially the Phoenicians), but also attracted invaders and attacks from those desiring to possess their land. The land produced a healthy supply of olives, grapes, grains, sheep, goats and some cattle.

In the earliest stage of the division, King Jeroboam ruled from the city of Shechem, a captured Canaanite town. Under later kings, the city of Samaria (later called Sebaste by Herod the Great) was the capital city of Israel (1 Kings 16:29) and was located in the territory of Manasseh. This capital city was first built (875BC) by King Omri, the sixth king of the divided kingdom

(1 Kings 16:24) and was completed by his son King Ahab. Samaria lasted till the Assyrian captivity (722BC) when it was destroyed, despite its strategic position, built like a stronghold on a hill (about 300 ft high). The city had both inner and outer walls with towers and bastions. Though its wall measured more than thirty feet wide and twenty feet high, it was no match for the Assyrian onslaught. The Israelite tribes of the region were conquered and led away during the Assyrian waves of invasion (C8 BCE). Settling in their place were the Samaritans, a sect still lives in the region today (though perhaps less than 1000 in total number).

With the return of the Jews from Babylonian captivity, the Samaritans and Jews did not have good relationships and were considered a mixed race by many Jews. During the rebuilding of the Temple, the Samaritans worked to prevent its completion (Ezra 4:1-10). During the rebuilding of the wall of Jerusalem, Nehemiah also had problems from the Samaritans, according to the Bible record (Nehemiah 2:10-6:14).

During the time of Alexander the Great, Samaria enjoyed some prosperity, with an investment in the city of Samaria as an important position as the Greek City of Israel. The region was for a while (330BC) a Macedonian colony and many of its people were deported as punishment for the murder of the appointed governor of Samaria. During this period, the region was dominated by a few forts and a regional city (Samaria) that was wholly Hellenistic in style. Several of these were captured and destroyed by John Hyrcanus (107 BCE) when he led the revolt in Judea. The region became part of the Roman Empire (63 BCE) with the arrival of Pompeii and was annexed into the province of Syria.

The chief city of the region was restored during this. The new regional capital city was built by Herod the Great (30 BCE). He made a new city wall, theater and a temple in Samaria in honor of Augustus Caesar and renamed the city Sebaste (Augustus in Greek). This was the city that stood in the time of Jesus and the Apostles. Some of the Roman ruins stand today.

Jesus went through Samaria where he met a Samaritan woman at a well and thereafter ministered in her town of Sychar for two days (John 4). Later, Jesus seemed to neglect the area in His active ministry, and instructed His disciples to go to the Jews only and to avoid the Gentile and Samaritan cities (Matthew 10:5).

In the book of Acts, the capital city of Samaria (Sebaste) was one of the towns that the Christians scattered to during the persecution that resulted after the stoning of Stephen (Acts 8:1). Philip is recorded to have gone to Samaria to preach there. The word of the Lord spread all over Samaria and the people received the power of the Holy Spirit upon them through the laying on of hands by Peter and John. The city is also mentioned as the place where Simon the magician lived.

Samaritans still exist in the area of Mount Gerizim (as their holy mountain) and strictly observe Sabbath, and offer sacrifices at their own observance of the Passover.

Samos (Island of)

Acts 20:15

The large east-west oriented island (27 miles east-west and about 14 miles north-south) is located southwest of ancient Ephesus in the Aegean Sea. It was an ancient Ionian settlement founded probably as early as the 11th century BCE, and was thought to be settled by the people of Epidaurus. The colony enjoyed great prosperity in the C6-5th BCE. The maritime colony developed healthy trade with the Asian coast.

The island passed to Rome through the will of the last Pergamene king (133 BCE). Under the Romans the island was severed from its client relationship to the mainland and given free status (by Augustus in 17 BCE). The island was known for its woolen products, pottery and fine metalwork. The island was home to several ancient poets and moralists like Anacreon, Aesop, Ibycus and the astronomer Cono.

Paul either "passed by" or "touched" the island in the channel between the island and mainland on his third mission journey. (Note the unusual use of the term *parebalomen* and the variety of its translations). Paul sailed from Assos to Mitylene, Chios and then by Samos, on his way to Jerusalem.

Samothracia (Island of)

Acts 16:11 (for a similar journey, see 20:6)

Visible from the coastal villages of Thrace (on a clear day), the mountain island of Samothracia is equidistant from the Turkish coast and Alexandropoli today. The small oval shaped island rises up dramatically from the Aegean, with a peak that rises above 1700 meters from the ocean surface. Paul passed by the island at least twice (probably several times more) in his various mission journeys. Following the Macedonian man's call for help (in the vision of Paul) the ship carrying the mission team harbored at the island for one night. This marked the beginning of the "we" sections of Luke's narrative, probably signaling that he joined the team at that time. A large temple complex overshadowed the harbor from the cliffs above, and there is no record of Paul disembarking the ship on this island, known for the mystery cult center of the Kabeiroi (fertility deities). If the temple were in use at the time (as most suppose) Paul may have heard the drum beat associated with the pagan rituals of the place.

Seleucia

Acts 13:4 (possibly also 14:26 and 15:30,39)

The seaport that was responsible for the tremendous wealth and expansion of Syrian Antioch was named after Seleucus Nicator I around 300 BCE. The port was founded first, then a trade route established, and finally the planting of a major city. Located a few miles from the mouth of the Orontes River, the flow of goods made their way the fifteen miles to Antioch. There may have been about 30,000 inhabitants during the time of Paul's travels. Paul and Joses Barnabas sailed from Seleucia to Cyprus on their First Mission Journey.

Sidon

Acts 12:20; 27:3; Genesis 10:15,19; 49:13; Joshua 19:28; Judges 1:31; I Kings 16:31; 2 Kings 23:13; Isaiah 23:12; Jeremiah 27; Ezekiel 20-24; Joel 3:6; Matthew 11:21,22; 15:21; Mark 3:8; 7:24,31; Luke 4:26; 6:17; 10:13,14;

The name "Sidon" is first mentioned in Genesis 10:15 as the first-born son of Canaan. Later the name is given in reference to a city in verse 19 on the border of the Canaanite territory. Traditionally, the city of Sidon was the first of the Phoenician strongholds (1 Chron. 1:13). Sidon, Tyre, Byblos and Aradus are thought by most scholars to have been the four most important towns of the Phoenicians. These cities were politically independent city-states and never united. The Sidonians and Tyrians (Tyre was a sister port) worshipped gods that were part of the common worship of the gods of fertility and harvest normally associated with the Phoenician cultic practice. For this reason (as well as scant literary references) most scholars accept the notion that it was a Phoenician city at its foundation.

Egyptian influence and domination was evident in the period of the 18th and 19th dynasties (see the article on the city of Acco for more on this). According to the Amarna tablet records, a ruler named Zimri-ada took the city from Egyptian control (circa. 1350 BCE). Sidon could not be conquered by the tribe of Asher and became a border of property allotted as her inheritance (Judges 1:31). Some believe the Sidonians attempted to gain the territory of Dor, an incursion that brought on a war with the Philistines (Peleste) and ended in Sidon's destruction.

Sidon was rebuilt and became a neighbor of Asher and Zebulun (Genesis 49:13; Joshua 19:28). The constant desire to expand gave Sidon the reputation of an oppressive neighbor to the tribes of Israel (Judges 10:12). The rule of King Ahab brought an alliance through marriage to Jezebel the daughter of Ethbaal (king of Sidon). This alliance brought the idolatry of Sidon. (Their chief gods were Baal (1 Kings 16:31) and Ashteroth (2 Kings 23:13). This caused additional moral and spiritual decay in Israel and was attributed to part of the rationale of the invasion and exile by the Assyrians.

Sidon and Tyre were closely linked over Biblical history as "sister cities" and often had a symbiotic relationship. Isaiah predicted judgement on Tyre and called her the daughter of Sidon (Isaiah 23:12). Ezekiel was commanded by the Lord to set his face toward Sidon and prophesy against it (Ezekiel 28:20-24). Jeremiah prophesied to all the kings of the nations including Sidon to be subject to the rule of Babylon for their preservation (Jeremiah 27).

The desire to expand caused trouble with the Assyrians, who eventually extracted a tribute from the Sidonians (circa. 880 BCE). The Assyrians bought much of their fleet from the Phoenician ports (Zech. 9:2). Assyrian records show great quantities of ivory given as tributes and gifts to the Assyrian kings. A generation later, Shalmaneser III brought his armies to the Dog River demanding more tribute. The scene was depicted on the temple gate at Balawat (and can be viewed in the British Museum). During the rise of Greek domination in the C4 BCE, Sidon attempted an uprising against Cyprus and the other Phoenician powers, and 40,000 were slaughtered and the city burned (350 BCE).

Sidonians were highly skilled artisans and tradesmen in the arts of carved ivory, silver and gold to decorate furniture and architecture. For a time Sidon led in the production of purple dye from murex snails (a labor intensive process). The extraction of red and purple dye (*phoinix* in Greek) gave the area its ancient name - Phoenicia. Schools for the philosophical disciplines (including the study of science, arithmetic, astronomy and law) as well as glass blowing were the Sidonian pursuits of the first century BCE. During the Roman period, Sidon enjoyed virtual independence for a time.

The chief shrine of the Sidon was the temple of Eshmun (the god of healing). This early healing center was well known (as were Asklepion in other places). It is ironic that among the few stories related during the visit of Jesus to the area of Tyre and Sidon (Matthew15: 21; Mark 7:24) was a healing on behalf of a request from a Syro-Phoenician woman. Jesus mentioned Tyre and Sidon (as synonymous with "pagans") when he declared that judgement would be "more tolerable for Tyre and Sidon than for Bethsaida and Chorazin", cities of Israel that rejected Him

(Matthew 11:21,22). People came from Tyre and Sidon to be healed by Jesus (Mark 3:8; Luke 6:17) when they found the worship of Eshmun ineffective.

In the Book of Acts, Tyre and Sidon are recorded to have sought peace with King Herod Agrippa I at the time of his death (Acts 12:20). Sidon was one of the port calls for the ship that carried Paul and the other prisoners on the way to Rome (Acts 27:3).

Modern Sidon is now a part of Lebanon, a modern city built over the ruins of the ancient city. Sometimes referred to as "Saida", it is thirty miles south of Beirut and about thirty miles north of Tyre.

Syracuse

Acts 28:12

Syracuse (modern Siracusa) is located on Sicily's eastern coast in the Mediterranean (due south of the Ionian) Sea. Historians note the city was established by Archias of Corinth along with Dorian and Corinthian settlers in 734 BCE. The large landmass of Sicily included settlements of tribes from as far away North Africa and the Phoenician coast. In Syracuse, the harbor town became very prosperous in the last part of the 5th century BCE. Under the tyrants Gelon and Dionysius I it grew to the status of the preeminent city of all Sicily. It withstood an Athenian attack in 415-413 BCE launched by frustrated generals of Athens that had been unable to defeat the Spartan armies after nearly fifteen years of on-going conflicts in Achaia. The successful defense of the port lead to a humiliating retreat by the Athenians and bolstered the reputation of the Sicilians as fighters. In the wake of the assault, the following century brought waves of immigrants including Carthaginians that fled the Roman advances into North Africa. Periodic conflicts developed between settlers from Phoenicia and the other Greeks on the northern and eastern end of the island and plagued the island until stopped by Roman involvement.

Despite the powerful defenses devised on a plan by the famed mathematician Archimedes, the city was seized by the overwhelming power of the Romans in 212 BCE. The Roman province of Sicily was formed, with Syracuse given the status of its' capital. The Roman governing system and economic ties brought prosperity that kept the city flourishing through the Roman Period (until about the C3 CE).

Though Paul's ship stopped over here, it is unknown whether he traversed on the island itself. Several traditions have developed, but are not confirmed by earliest sources. It is thought they were here for three days awaiting a good breeze to drive them northward, though they were possibly taking care of other needed business for they had been on Melita for three months (Acts 28:11).

Syria (Region)

Acts 15:23, 41; 18:18; 20:3; 21:3. Antioch (of Syria): Acts 6:5; 11:19, 20, 22, 26, 27; 13:1; 14:26; 15:22,23,30,35; 18:22. Seleucia: Acts 13:4. Damascus: Acts 9:2,3,8,10,19,22,27: 22:5,6,10,11; 26:12, 20

Originally called *Aram* in Hebrew because of the nomadic Aramaeans who lived in this area by the 12th century BCE. (Some scholars suggest the term could have also been the Hurrian name applied to the Semites who came from across the Tigris, and eventually settled in the Syrian and Northwestern Mesopotamia region. Whether Aram was their own Semitic tribal name or a name attached to them by others is uncertain). Ancient Greek historians used the term Syria, a possible shortened name derived from the Babylonian name *Suri*.

Like many areas around the Mediterranean, Syria's early borders are hard to define. It was located south of the Taurus Mountain Range, northeast of Israel and tucked between the vast desert plateau in the east and the Mediterranean Sea to its west. Two significant parallel mountain ranges include Mt. Hermon lying in the western range while Mt. Cassius was in the east. Three important rivers, the Jordan, Orontes and Leontes watered the Coele Syria plain, which was located between the eastern and western ranges, while water from northern Syria also fed into the Euphrates.

By the time of the Kings of Israel the Aramaeans had many rulers, making several small kingdoms, some of whom David fought and defeated, though under Solomon's rule they regained some power as Israel's military strength was weakened. Later, king Asa of Judah (911-876) allied with Ben-ha-dad of Syria who broke his treaty with king Baasha of Israel (909-886) and defeated him in many areas (1 Kings 15:16-21). Israel and Judah had many other confrontations with Syria afterwards, some to and some against their advantage (1 Kings 20:1-34; 2 Kings 8:28-29; 10:32-33; 13:24-25; 14:28; 16:5; Isa. 7:1).

Later, Syria went from the possession of the Persians to Alexander the Great to the Seleucids whose kingdom, at one point, stretched further eastward even to include Babylon. It became a Roman province in 64 BCE and its borders went southward all the way from the Taurus Mountains in the north to Egypt in the south, and eastward to the Euphrates from the Mediterranean Sea.

Paul visited this region many times during his Christian ministry. It was also on his way to Syrian Damascus that Paul met the risen Savior and stayed in the city. He first began to preach the Gospel there (9:20). Within the territory of ancient Syria was the great city of Antioch on the Orontes River, where believers were first known as Christians (11:26). It was also a spiritual home for Paul, the city where he set out each of his important missionary journeys (13:3; 15:40; 18:23). Seleucia is only mentioned once and is a city from which Paul sailed, heading to Cyprus with Barnabas, on the First Missionary Journey (13:4).

Tarsus

(Acts 7:58; 9:11, 30; 11:25; 21:39; 22:3; 22:28; 26:9-10; Rom. 11:1; 2 Cor. 11:22; Gal. 1:14; Phil. 3:4-7; 2 Tim. 3:14ff)

Tarsus was the capital of the Roman Province of Cilicia (cp. Acts 22:3), situated between the Taurus Mountains and the Mediterranean Sea. The Province of Cilicia varied between 30 to 60 miles wide and was about 300 miles long. The city of Tarsus was about 10 miles inland of the Mediterranean on the alluvial plain, watered by the Cydnus and may have had as many as one half million inhabitants in the time of Paul. Ramsey described the city as about 70 feet above sea level on a level plain. The lower Cyndus was made navigable and a port had been built to carry goods to and from the sea. A major road lead to the north where the famous mountain pass known as the "Cilician Gates" lay less than 29 miles inland. Sir William Ramsey described the pass as "one of the most famous and important passes in history".

The origins of the city are shrouded in mystery, but it appears the city was a native Cilician town taken over by Ionian settlers of antiquity. Josephus attributes the city to the Tarshish of Genesis 10:4, but this is by no means certain. It is mentioned several places in historical record with certainty. The Black Obelisk of Shalmaneser says this city was taken by the Assyrians (mid C9 BCE). Xenophon passed through in 401 BCE, and found the ruler to be a local. Alexander found the rulership in the hands of the Persians, and he replaced the ruler (334 BCE).

Coins found in excavations of the region make no claim of autonomy until after the defeat of Antiochus the Great at the hands of the Romans (189 BCE). Syria appears to have undergone some reorganization at this time, allowing autonomy in some of the regions. Tarsus appears to have grown into autonomy at this time establishing a constitution as a free city. The city became part of the Roman Empire with the arrival of Pompey the Roman General and the defeat of the pirates that often harassed the city by about 64 BCE.

Some scholars speculate that Paul may be a descendant of some of those who were promised free citizenship if they moved to the Cilician city in 171 BCE. Another claim for the citizenship ancestry of Paul can be found in some who raise the possibility that Paul's father or grandfather helped Marc Antony (and thus Rome) during Cleopatra's renowned visit to Tarsus in 41 BCE. The historian Strabo mentions the splendor of the event, as Cleopatra sailed her gilded barge in the Cyndus into the city. In addition, there is reason to believe that Antony and Octavian used some resources of the city in their struggle against Brutus and Cassius, who they later defeated at Philippi in Macedonia. Some have even suggested that a tent maker's gift could have been repaid in citizenship (cp. Acts 18:3), though this is mere speculation.

Autonomy meant that Tarsus was able to govern itself under its own laws, impose import taxation and a variety of other freedoms. Strabo mentions that the city was excited by education, and was home to the third largest university, after Athens and Alexandria. One teacher or note that came from Tarsus was the famous Athenodorus, a Stoic Philosopher that tutored Augustus at Apollonia, and later became his advisor from 44 to 15 BCE. This probably accounts for August's favor on the city. Athenodorus returned to Tarsus and established a reform to the city in15 BCE. Along with the reforms, he established a patrician class that probably included the family of Paul, who boasts of his association with the city (Acts 21:39).

In addition to being the hometown of Paul (Acts 9:11; 21:39; 22:3), it was also the city Paul returned to after his escape from Jerusalem (Acts 9:30). Barnabas found Paul in the city and enlisted him to service at Antioch (Acts 11:25ff). Paul may well have visited on the Second and Third Mission Journeys (Acts 15:41; 18:22-23).

The fair havens

Acts 27:8

This small harbor of the south central coast of Crete has been identified with the bay east of Cape Littinos (also called locally Cape Matala). The modern seaside village of Kali Limenes lies at the end of a small country road, and belies the once significant harbor area of the Roman period. Few remains are restored. Only a small Byzantine chapel dedicated to Paul has been maintained to recall Paul's time in the harbor. The chapel was mentioned by a naval officer who traveled the area (Captain T.A.B. Spratt, *Travels and Researches in Crete* [1865], II 1-6).

The harbor opened toward the east and was sheltered on the southwest by two small islands. In winter, southwest winds make the harbor quite rough, one reason the ship carrying Paul continued on with its fateful journey. The ship was likely in less danger in the harbor than to pass the cape and take on the northwest winds, a fact they came to understand after leaving. Perhaps the vulnerability of ships to piracy (the area was not completely secure until a few years after Paul's journeys) also led to the decision to depart.

Thessalonica

Acts 17:1, 11,13; 27:2; Philippians 4:16; 2 Timothy 4:10;

The port city of Thessalonica (now called Salonica or Thessaloniki) was founded by the Macedonian General Kassander in celebration of the successful campaigns against the Persians (315 BCE). With the triumphs and expansion of their influence, new wealth poured into Macedonia and allowed new settlements to be established. This port was constructed on the Thermaic Gulf and knitted together twenty-six villages (including a village called "Thermae" by Herodotus - C5 BCE in his book Polymnia –the description of Xerxes expedition against Greece) as the main seaport and naval base of Macedonia. The original villages were Doric settlements of the period of Macedonian Kings (C5-4 BCE). The new city was named after his wife (Thessalonike, daughter of Philip II and half sister of Alexander the Great).

As the successor of Alexander the Great, Kassander had considerable resources. He erected a massive wall around the city. The position of the city only improved with the completion of the "Egnatian Way" which made the port easily accessible to other Macedonian cities. The "Via Egnatia" ran through the city and can still be seen today. Strabo the geographer (C1 BCE) in "Geographic Elements" referred to the port as the "Metropolis of Macedonia".

The Celts attacked the city and smashed many of the defenses and walls (during the battle in which Ptolemaeus – "the Thunderbolt" was killed) but were turned back by the defenders of the town. Even the Romans were repelled in their early advances, but the city was surrendered after Perseus (King of Macedonia) was defeated at Pydna in 168 BCE. Under the Roman Empire, Thessalonica became the capital city of the Roman province of Macedonia (146 BCE). The city was referred to as the "Mother of Macedonia" in Roman writings. The orator Cicero stayed here and delivered oratory. With the rise of the Roman Civil War (49-31 BCE) Thessalonica backed Antony and

Octavian (who stayed in Thessalonica after their victory). Later, the "Gate of Axous" (arch) was erected to commemorate victory at the Battle of Philippi (42 BCE). Octavian declared Thessalonica a "free city" under Politarchs (Magistrates).

Thessalonica was a wealthy city and had a Roman, Greek and Jewish population. After 42 BCE, Thessalonica enjoyed liberty as a free city with a large population. Paul used the city as a gateway to reach the region. Recent excavations uncovered mile markers that say Thessalonica was the halfway point in the travel along the Via Egnatia (they said there was a distance of 260 Roman miles in either direction to end points).

Paul came to Thessalonica from Philippi (probably in 50 CE). He went to the synagogue for three Sabbath days (Acts 17:1-9). In Thessalonica, some proselyte Greeks and the chief women believed Paul's preaching. The Jews who did not believe caused uproar in the city and assaulted the house of Jason in order to bring out Paul and Silas. The people took Jason (Paul's host) and other believers to the rulers, accusing Jason of harboring traitors to Caesar. Jason and the other brethren were given a bond on the agreement that Paul would leave the area. Paul and Silas were sent away immediately by night to Berea. The decree of Claudius that expelled Jews from Rome was probably broadcast to the people along the Via Egnatia at about the time of Paul's visit. The Politarchs of the city were no doubt forced to act against Paul.

The preaching of the gospel in Thessalonica was very important and facilitated the spreading of the faith to all of Macedonia (1 Thessalonians 1:8). From Paul's letters to the Thessalonians it was evident that their faith was known throughout the region. They were a group of believers Paul remembered with great love and commendation in his letters. Aristachus and Secundus (of Thessalonica) believers labored with Paul (Acts 20:4; 27:2).

After his departure, Paul sent Timothy to Thessalonica. The First and Second Epistles to the Thessalonians were written in Corinth after Timothy offered a good report concerning the welfare of the church. Paul may have revisited Thessalonica and mentions his intention to visit in his letter to the Corinthians (1 Corinthians 16:5). This church suffered persecution (1

Thessalonians 2:14). Other important figures of the Thessalonians included Jason, Gaius, Secundus, Aristarchus and perhaps Demas (Acts 19:29; 20:4).

The "Three Taverns"

Acts 28:15

Only mentioned once in the Bible, fellow believers from Rome met Paul at the *Tres Tabernae* (Latin), when they heard he was coming to their city. This village was located approximately 30 miles (50 km.) from Rome. Some scholars believe the name could also be properly translated as "Three Shops". The location was a crossroad connecting Antium and Norba with the Appian Way, which led to Rome.

The Appian Way or "Via Appia" was built around 312 BCE to connect Rome to Capua. Later (by 244 BCE) it was expanded all the way to Brundisium, located approximately 350 miles from Rome. From Brundisium, travelers could cross the Adriatic to Dyrrachium and continue through Macedonia to Philippi along the Egnatian Way. Sections of the Appian Way have still been used even in modern times.

Troas

(Acts 16:6-10; 20:7-12; 2 Cor. 2:12-13)

The principal seaport in northwest Asia Minor with an artificially engineered harbor to shelter boats from the prevailing northern winds. The site was established about 11 miles from the historic city of Troy (Illium). Strabo refers to the city as "one of the notable cities of the world". The harbor was a launching site for many boats ferrying people and goods to Neapolis (modern Kavalla), to begin their land journey to Rome. Emperor Augustus made it a Roman colony, and it served as a strategic point on the east west communication route.

After the split with Barnabas, Paul and Silas proceeded to visit the churches of the First Mission Journey in Syria and Cilicia, and then on into southern Galatia (Acts 15:36-41) carrying the message of the Jerusalem Council to the churches. Eventually they headed west toward Europe. Stopping at Troas, Paul appeared to desire to turn north into the regions of upper Galatia, but received the vision of the "Macedonian Man" at Troas. He later described the experience as "a door opening in the Lord" (2 Cor. 2:12ff). This occurred during this Second Mission Journey (Acts 16:6-10). Years later he returned to Troas from his more than two year stay in Ephesus (Acts 19:8,10) toward the end of the Third Mission Journey, before continuing on to Assos. During the last seven-day stay at Troas, the fallen Eutychus was healed (Acts 20:8-12). The team took the boat to around Cape Lectum to Assos, but Paul chose rather to journey the 20 miles on foot, perhaps desiring a rare time of solitude.

Some suggest that Paul's urgent request to return a cloak he left in Troas (2 Timothy 4:13) may have reflected that Paul's departure from the city was hurried. Later church history recalls the reference to Ignatius, after writing three Epistles at Troas, set sail under arrest to Rome. The site is abandoned today, with only a few monumental walls intact. A stadium, a gymnasium, some of the city walls, and the harbor can be outlined.

Trogyllium

Acts 20:15

Trogyllium was located due west of ancient Priene along a cape south opposite Samos Island. The city was located about half way between Ephesus and Miletus. The city guarded the west coast of Asia Minor and the shipping lane in the Strait of Samos. Though a nearly two-kilometer passage, the narrow strait was not easily navigable in darkness before the modern buoys and lighting systems. Likely the captain of the vessel during the travels of Paul did not want to risk a night passage. Paul was on his way to Jerusalem during his Third Mission Journey and had a brief stop at Trogyllium before he continued to Miletus, Coos (Kos), Rhodes and eventually the port city of Tyre.

Tyre

Acts 12:20; 21:3,7; Joshua 19:29; II Samuel 5:11; 24:7; II Samuel 5:11; I Kings 5:1; 7:13,14; 9:11,12; I Chronicles 14:1; 22:4; II Chronicles 2:3,11,14; Ezra 3:7; Nehemiah 13:16; Psalm

45:12; 83:7; 87:4; Isaiah 23:1,5,8,15,17; Ezekiel 26:27; Joel 3:4; Matthew 11:21, 22; 15:21; Mark 3:8; 7:24, 31; Luke 6:17; 10:13,14

Tyre (modern "Sur") was the principal port of the Phoenicians twenty-eight miles (40 km.) south of Sidon and eighteen miles north of the natural ridge border with Israel. A small island off the coast of the natural harbor was incorporated into the city in antiquity and the city offered twin ports, with a city divided by waterway. Tyre had natural defenses with mountains due east and the sea west. The rocky cliffs acted as a barrier. In spite of the defenses, Tyre was an attractive port for local goods. Ships with cargo bound inland normally stopped at Sidon (because the inland travel was easier). Tyre has been recorded as a "daughter of Sidon" (Isaiah 23:2,12).

Herodotus (2.44) records Tyre was founded in about 2700 BCE. It was referred to in several ancient texts, including the Execration Texts (1850 BCE) from Egypt, Ras Shamra tablets (1450 BCE), and a Canaanite poem. It is amply represented in the Akkadian language of the Amarna tablets (1350 BCE), where the ruler complained to Amenophis III of the troubles in the region. In the Hebrew Scriptures, the stronghold acted as a border fortress to Asher and was referred to as a "fortress". (Joshua 19:29; 2 Samuel 24:7). Egyptian decline left Tyre a virtually independent city-state by the time of King David. King Hiram I, a friend of David, supplied materials for the Temple construction in Jerusalem during the reign of both David and Solomon. According to the Bible, Hiram sent both cedar wood and craftsmen to them (2 Samuel 5:11; 1 Kings 5:1). Later, book of Isaiah records a whole of chapter (23) dedicated to Tyre - her judgement and her restoration. In that period (sometimes called the "golden age of Tyre") the trading power of the port was evident, as she is called a merchant city (Isaiah 23:11). Tyre was much known for the exports of timber, the purple dye and murex-dyed cloth (called "Tyrian"), tin and tin ore, worked silver and copper. The city was not in an agricultural basin and thus traded with neighbors for her agricultural needs.

After the period of Hiram, the city fell victim to a number of coups and troubles that weakened her economically. Two generations after Hiram the ruler (Abid Astarte, 'Servant of the

Ashtarote god') was murdered by his brother. Some time later, the high priest Ethbaal (father of Jezebel of Israel) overthrew King Astaymus (circa 897 BCE). Some scholars believe the success of Ethbaal in the coup was due in part to the work of the Assyrian Ashurbanipal II (working behind the scenes). The increasing pressure of high tribute payments to Assyria eventually stripped the vitality of the economy in the Phoenician cities. At least six times the tribute reportedly exacted a heavy toll on the city. Some merchants longed to move from the grasp of Assyrian, and Tyre founded a colony in northern Africa at Carthage by 815 BCE.

As with Sidon, Tyre was the subject of prophecies of judgement. Amos condemned her for handing over the Israelites to the Edomites. Joel condemned both Tyre and Sidon for selling the Israelites to the Greeks. Ezekiel also prophesied the destruction of Tyre (Ezekiel 26:3-21). Shalmenezzar V of Assyria laid a siege of the port, and it was destroyed about the time of the fall of Samaria. Tyre was restored and heavy tribute was exacted to Nineveh. With the aid of Egypt, the city disrupted the flow of tribute on several occasions. The city was later besieged for thirteen years (according to Josephus in Antiquities) and destroyed by Nebuchadnezzar II of Babylon (585-572 BCE). Her port was besieged again for seven months by Alexander the Great with the help of Sidon (332 BCE). Alexander aided in the restoration of the port soon after he took it.

During the Roman Empire, Tyre was rebuilt and restored to prosperity. It was named a Roman colony. By the time of the visit of Jesus to the region, the chief temple of the city was restored (with money from Herod the Great). Jesus visited the region. The inhabitants knew Him as some came from Tyre and Sidon to listen to His teachings and witness healings (Mt. 15:21-28; Mark 7:24-31). In the Book of Acts, Tyre was one of the ports of call for Paul during his third missionary journey on his way to Jerusalem. He stayed there for seven days with disciples who warned him by the Holy Spirit not to go to Jerusalem (Acts 21:2-7). The Christian community continued to thrive there, and Origen was later buried there (254 CE).

Made in the USA
Monee, IL
11 September 2023

42545773R00066